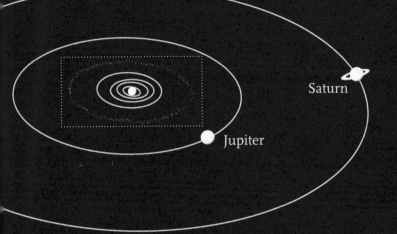

Saturn

Jupiter

Uranus

Neptune

BEYOND

A SOLAR SYSTEM VOYAGE

BEY

O n D

A SOLAR SYSTEM VOYAGE

MICHAEL BENSON

ABRAMS BOOKS FOR YOUNG READERS

NEW YORK

6-17-09

CONTENTS

INTRODUCTION

S ince the earliest days of the human race, people
have observed the sky with a mixture of fascination and wonder. Long before electric lights kept
our attention artificially on what's near and familiar at the
expense of what's far away and mysterious, we wondered
about the glinting stars and planets, as well as about the
Moon and Sun.

Many theories have existed about the meaning of what
we could see of the Universe from our position on Earth.
Most of these ideas are lost to us, because they were developed by the earliest human beings before written records
were kept. But we know enough about ourselves to guess
that even when our earliest ancestors observed the night
sky, they already had the curiosity, the imagination, and the
mental capacity to construct theories and beliefs about it.

Of course we still stargaze when we can. Although the
stars and planets above the brightly lit cities of our 21st-

OPPOSITE **Throughout history,
human beings have tried to
comprehend the mysterious
workings of the cosmos. The
name of this painting, by D. Owen
Stephens, is *The Astronomer*.**

This famous illustration of a medieval pilgrim peering through the sky to try to determine the inner workings of the Universe is an excellent depiction of that timeless human drive. When it first appeared in 1888, it was published with an inscription: "What, then, is this blue sky, which certainly does exist, and which veils from us the stars during the day?"

century civilization can be much harder for us to see with our own eyes, when we get away from all that illumination, many hundreds of glittering lights are still visible in the sky on a clear night. And we now have some remarkable tools, devices that our ancestors could only dream about, to help us investigate the skies. Among them is a quite recent invention: the space probe, or unmanned spacecraft. Almost all the pictures in this book were taken by them. After more than 50 years of such space missions, we now know a lot more about the planets than our ancestors did. Yet we're still just beginning to understand these very distant places.

Rather than starting from the central Sun and moving outward from there to examine the planets in order of their distance from it (Mercury, Venus, Earth, Mars, Jupiter,

Saturn, Uranus, and Neptune), *Beyond* examines the Solar System from the perspective of these robot explorers. This "trajectory" (the path a projectile makes through space) goes as follows: the Earth-Moon System, Venus, the Sun, Mercury, Mars, the asteroids, the Jupiter System, Saturn, Uranus, and Neptune.

Why do we "fly" this way? One reason is that it seemed logical to begin at our home world and our satellite, the Moon—the first worlds we photographed from space—and then go on a longer journey. And it also seemed right to

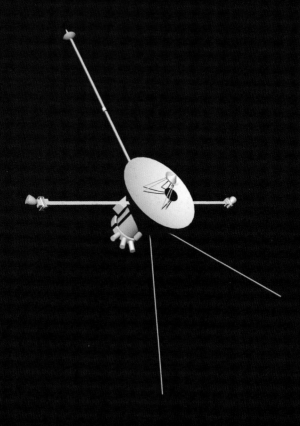

The school bus–size Cassini Orbiter was launched in 1997, arrived at its destination of Saturn on July 1, 2004, and continues to send back invaluable information about that planet, its rings, and its moons.

begin that trip by following the actual history of our robotic explorations: after the Moon, we first visited the Inner Planets (Mercury, Venus, and Mars). It was Venus that was the first place we successfully sent a robot to explore, with Mars and Mercury coming not so long after. The giant Outer Planets—Jupiter, Saturn, Uranus, and Neptune—were only visited later, including when the two spectacular Voyager missions of the 1970s and 1980s took advantage of an unusual alignment of these "gas giants" and flew past all four of them.

But there's another reason why I chose this structure for *Beyond*. Because it takes so much rocket power to send a space probe to Jupiter or Saturn directly from Earth, NASA specialists in the late 1980s figured out an unusual and indirect—but very energy-efficient—way to do it. Their solution was to send such spacecraft first toward Venus—meaning closer to the Sun—before the probe returned to fly past the Earth again on the way to the Outer Solar System. The planners at NASA did this to take advantage of the fact that a spacecraft picks up speed every time it flies past an object as large as a planet. In a sense, each flyby works like a slingshot, with the gravitational attraction of the planet acting as the *arm* and the spacecraft itself as the *rock being slung*. In this way, quite large space probes can be sent to Jupiter and Saturn with relatively small rocket engines. Two of them are depicted on these pages.

Although it includes pictures from many missions across 50 years of space exploration, this book follows that indirect—but useful—inward-outward trajectory. It, too, travels from the Earth toward Venus and the blazing Sun before flying past Mercury and Mars—the rest of the rocky "terrestrial" worlds of the Inner Solar System—on its way to explore the gas giant planets of the Outer Solar System and their moons. Why is Mercury after the Sun, rather than before it? Because, according to my concept, both Mercury and Mars happened to be on the far side of the Sun from the Earth and Venus at the time our picture-happy spacecraft was launched.

With its emphasis on the visual, *Beyond* is not meant to be a detailed study of the many astonishing scientific discoveries we've made along the way. Rather, this book provides a photographic introduction to the astonishingly diverse landscapes that wheel like a giant clockwork around our central star, the Sun. *Beyond* seeks to make an argument that the visual harvest of these unmanned space missions belongs as much to the history of photography as it does to the history of science. So if the text sometimes seems to take a backseat to the pictures, it is only appropriate. And if *Beyond* conveys some of what these strange and beautiful places would look like to someone lucky enough to see them glimmering through the windows of an interplanetary spaceship, then the book has succeeded.

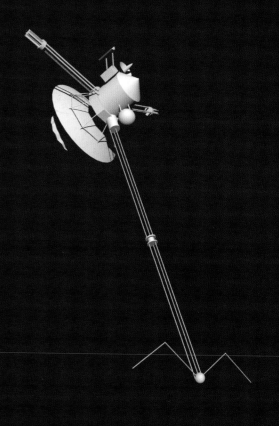

The Galileo Orbiter arrived at Jupiter in late 1995 and spent eight years investigating the Solar System's largest planet and its diverse moons.

CHAPTER I

THE LONG PATH
TO THE PLANETS

F or most of human history, people wandered across the landscape of our planet, hunting and gathering plants, fruit, and nuts as they went. We call this period, which lasted for hundreds of thousands of years, prehistory. "Prehistory" simply means that we have very little information about what happened then, but of course it doesn't mean that history wasn't actually unfolding at the time. In fact, a slow accumulation of knowledge and skills was being passed on from parent to child as the centuries passed. Not until about 6,000 years ago did humans start to settle down in permanent settlements and cultivate plants and farm animals. One of the places we know they did this was in Mesopotamia, in what we now call the Middle East. Between 5,000 and 6,000 years ago, Mesopotamians invented the first known writing. Called cuneiform, it was done by pressing a tool into damp clay tablets, which then dried. Since Mesopotamians recorded

their history in this way, we can read what they left behind. This is when prehistory became history. We have actual information, and we are not just making assumptions.

Mesopotamians were very interested in observing the sky—and because of cuneiform, they were able to record their observations. As a result, we think they developed a much more sophisticated understanding of the regular movements they saw in the skies than did previous cultures. (Not much later, perhaps even at the same time, the astronomers of China and India were also busy recording the movements they saw in the night sky.)

One Mesopotamian kingdom, Babylon, was particularly advanced in studying the skies. Babylonians became the first real astronomers. (Astronomers are scientists who study the planets and stars.) The Babylonian astronomers learned to predict eclipses. An eclipse is when the Moon passes in front of the Sun, creating a shadow on the Earth;

or when the shadow of the Earth passes across the Moon. Babylonian astronomers also knew about solstices, which in winter is when the days stop getting shorter and start getting longer again. In summer, the pattern is reversed, with days lengthening and then becoming shorter. They created the first 12-month calendar, based on the cycles of the Moon. They divided the year into seasons, and they also developed an elaborate religious belief system based on the motions of the planets and stars.

The observations of the Babylonian astronomers became the foundation of the work of all the later astronomers, at least in the Western world. People had known for a long time that a few of the stars in the sky seem to wander; they don't stay in the same positions in relation to other stars or to each other. Later the Greeks called the five visible wandering stars "planets." (The word means "wanderer" in ancient Greek.)

The five planets they recognized are Jupiter, Venus, Saturn, Mercury, and Mars. The repetitive motions of these visible planets, as well as those of the Moon and Sun, were already understood as a very useful way to mark the time. In fact, archaeological evidence tells us that many prehistoric cultures showed an ability to measure the motions they saw in the heavens. But the Babylonians took this knowledge many steps further. They created the seven-day week we still use today, and named its days after the five planets, plus the Sun and Moon. (For example, Sunday is still named after the Sun and Monday after the Moon.)

The Babylonians had no clear understanding that the

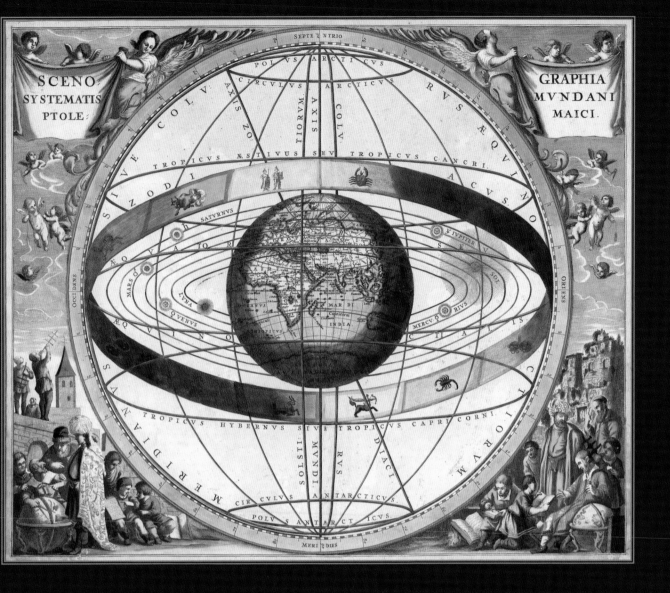

planets might be worlds comparable to our own. They just knew that they were wandering points of light. But this made them somehow special. Their *cyclical* or repetitive movements, as well as those of the Sun and Moon, made it possible to know exactly when the best time to plant seeds was and when to harvest the resulting crops. This was very important information, because it could make the difference between having enough food or not, and this in turn could determine the survival or failure of an entire kingdom or civilization. Is it any wonder that the

OPPOSITE After reading of the radical ideas of ancient Greek astronomer Aristarchus, Polish astronomer Nicolaus Copernicus correctly saw that the Sun must be at the center of the planets—not Earth. His first assertions to this effect were in a handwritten six-page document distributed to his friends in 1514. This image from a star atlas called the *Harmonia Macrocosmica*, published in 1660, depicts a Sun-centered Universe.

Babylonians developed a belief system regarding the power of the planets to affect human destinies (which today we call astrology)? Their observations would eventually lead to the creation of the clock and later the watch. (In fact, every circular clock face you see today is a simplification of the circular models of the Solar System originally based on Babylonian observations.)

The last stages of Babylonian astronomy took place about 2,000 years ago, when most of the Middle East was included in a Greek empire called the Seleucid Empire. Aristarchus of Samos, one of the astronomers from the early days of that empire, developed an interesting theory. Aristarchus studied Babylonian astronomy and observed the night sky. He was aware that an earlier Greek thinker named Philolaus, who lived around 400 B.C., once had the revolutionary idea that the Earth was not at the center of the Universe. Philolaus, however, didn't give a satisfying explanation as to what *was* at the center. Working between 310 and 230 B.C., Aristarchus took this thought much further. He wrote that the Sun must be at the center, with the planets revolving around it. He also put the visible planets in their correct order from the Sun: Mercury, Venus, Earth, Mars, Jupiter, and Saturn.

Another Babylonian astronomer, Seleucus, agreed with Aristarchus's theory, but the idea proved too radical to catch on, and was largely forgotten. Instead, Greek thinkers such as Plato and Aristotle mistakenly believed that the Earth was at the center of the Universe. In their model of the heavens, which was *geocentric*, or Earth-centered, the Moon,

Greeks even thought that the stars and planets were carried around the Earth by being embedded in a set of rotating spheres made of a kind of clear element that they called "quintessence." In fact, nearly 2,000 years passed before Aristarchus's Sun-centered, or *heliocentric*, model for the Universe was revived.

Although the idea that the Earth is at the center of everything may seem strange, it's not that hard to see how such a model of the heavens might have made sense at the time. After all, to us much as to the ancient Greeks, it appears that the Earth under our feet is solid and unmoving. Meanwhile, objects in the sky look like they're moving around the Earth at various rates. To this day, we speak of the Sun and Moon "setting" and "rising." So Aristarchus and Seleucus, two almost forgotten Greek geniuses, were simply ahead of their time. Very far ahead.

The geocentric model of the heavens devised by Plato and Aristotle was adopted by the Romans and later civilizations. About 2,000 years ago in Egypt, the astronomer Ptolemy adopted their incorrect model— although he also did later astronomers a great service by compiling much ancient astronomical knowledge in a book called the *Almagest*. It is the only surviving ancient *treatise*, or scientific text, on astronomy. Following the rise of Christianity, geocentrism (today called the Ptolemaic theory, after Ptolemy) was adopted by the Roman Catholic Church, in part because it worked well with their belief that humanity was at the center of the Universe. The church even branded anybody who disagreed with this view a *heretic*—meaning a disagreeable or even dangerous person. It was not a good thing to be called a heretic. Such people were jailed, and sometimes even killed. In any case, although they were wrong about the design of the Universe, Plato, Aristotle, and Ptolemy were three of the greatest thinkers ever. Their many other accurate contributions to science made their views on the heavens that much more believable to their contemporaries and those who followed.

Not until about 500 years ago, in 1514, did our view of how the Universe is designed begin to change for good. That was when Polish astronomer Nicolaus Copernicus, who had read of Aristarchus's ideas when he was studying ancient astronomical writings, developed a new model. Like Aristarchus's, it was heliocentric. Copernicus demonstrated clearly that the motions of the planets in the sky could be explained without the Earth being at the center. At first, he outlined this idea in a handwritten document he shared only with friends. Partly because he may have worried about how the Catholic Church would react, not until 30 years later, when he was dying, did he publish his most important work, *De Revolutionibus Orbium Coelestium* (*On the Revolutions of the Celestial Spheres*). It is one of the most important scientific documents ever published, and this treatise started what became known as the Copernican revolution.

Although Copernicus's heliocentric model was directly contradicted by some passages in the Bible (which says, "The Lord set the earth on its foundations; it can never be moved"), the Catholic Church didn't do anything about it—not at first. Not until almost 60 years later did it decide to "correct" Copernicus's book. The church did this mostly because of the actions of one man who would change the science of astronomy forever. His name was Galileo Galilei.

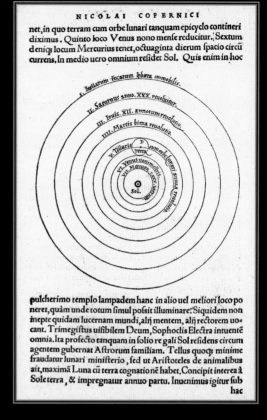

During the winter of 1609–1610, Italian astronomer
Galileo Galilei became the first to use a telescope to observe
the night sky. This instrument, a fairly simple tube with
lenses at each end, had been invented the previous year
in Holland. Based on a written description, Galileo built
his own. Instead of using it only to examine objects here
on Earth, as the Dutch had, he immediately started using
his telescope to watch the heavens. When he did, our

In December 1609, Galileo went outside and pointed his telescope at the Moon. What he saw astonished him. He saw mountains, which seemed to indicate that the Moon was a place much like the Earth. It also had strange circular forms all over it, which he named "craters"—after the ancient Greek word for *bowl*. In January 1610, he observed Jupiter and became the first human being ever to see that it was shaped like a sphere: not just a point of light, but clearly a real world. He also noticed three stars, strung out in a line next to the planet. But when he observed Jupiter over the next few nights, there were four, and they stayed with the planet as it moved across the sky from night to night. As time passed, they also exchanged positions, and they sometimes even seemed to vanish! Galileo concluded that these couldn't be stars. They must be moons much like our own planet's, and their disappearance was the result of their passing behind Jupiter.

When Galileo observed Venus, he saw that it slowly went through different phases like the Moon. It was completely illuminated at some times, looking full and round, while at others appearing as a crescent. Galileo's findings gave clear evidence that Copernicus's ideas were probably right. If Jupiter also had moons rotating around it, didn't it make sense that the planets themselves rotated around the Sun, just as Copernicus had predicted? And if Venus went through phases over time, then it, too, must be circling the Sun—its only source of light—rather than revolving around the Earth.

In March 1610, Galileo published his first conclusions in a short book, *The Starry Messenger*. It created a sensation and became the first science bestseller. Because Galileo's ideas and observations contradicted a few lines in the Bible and questioned the idea that humanity was at the center of the Universe, his theories eventually brought him into a direct confrontation with the powerful Catholic Church. When he published other books defending Copernicus's heliocentric theory, this controversy only increased. In 1633, when he was 69 years old, Galileo was ordered to Rome by the Catholic Church to stand trial on suspicion of being a heretic. He was found guilty, and he was ordered to say that he'd been wrong all along. Since not doing so would probably have meant that he would be killed, he did as he was told. Galileo was then placed under house arrest. He stayed in his home near Florence for the rest of his life.

But his achievements remain. Galileo's telescope revealed the planets to be real places—worlds in their own right—even if in the 1600s it was hard to dream that human beings would ever have a way to visit them. In this way, the telescope became the first instrument to help us start our journey into space, and it also made it possible for astronomy to become a modern science. After Galileo, a long line of great astronomers used increasingly powerful telescopes to observe the planets. Those sky gazers enabled us to see much farther, so more worlds were discovered: first Uranus in 1781, then Neptune in 1846. Gradually, humanity also became aware that, just as the Universe doesn't rotate around the Earth, so, too, it does not revolve around the Sun. Rather, the Sun is only one of countless stars, and our Solar System rotates around the glowing center of a vast, swirling mass of them called the Milky Way Galaxy. And this spiral collection of billions of suns—many of them, perhaps even most of them, containing their own system of planets—in turn isn't particularly special on the scale of the larger Universe. By the 1920s, astronomers were able to prove that the Milky Way itself is just one of many galaxies. How many? Nobody knows, but the figure is on the order of a hundred billion. Now we know there's no center to the Universe—just galaxies going on and on, seemingly forever.

As a result of the revelation that the planets are worlds and not wandering stars, many theories about them developed. Although we couldn't go there ourselves, our imaginations—now fueled by more information than ever before—went ahead of us. In 1944, toward the end of the Second World War, the Germans developed the first ballistic missile, the V-2. They used it primarily to bombard London. Although a weapon, it was the first man-made object to achieve suborbital spaceflight—meaning that although the V-2 didn't go into orbit and fully circle the Earth, it did leave our planet's atmosphere before coming back down. After the war, both the Soviet Union and the United States used V-2s as the basis for their own missile programs. Although they were developed for military reasons, the Soviets used one of their new multi-stage rockets in 1957 to launch the first Earth-orbiting satellite, Sputnik.

Because the United States and the Soviet Union saw themselves as enemies, Sputnik caused something like a panic in the United States. The launch of the first satellite proved that the Russians were ahead of the United States technologically—at least when it came to rockets. That was very hard for Americans to swallow. (Why call the Soviets "the Russians"? Because Russia was the biggest and most influential part of the Soviet Union.) This was a time of cold war between the United States and the Soviet Union; even though the two countries were competing fiercely, they weren't actually fighting. After Sputnik, U.S. president Dwight Eisenhower formed the U.S. space agency, the National Aeronautics and Space Administration, or NASA, in 1958. Its purpose was to compete with the Russians in space. Not long after, in April 1961, the Soviet Union launched Yuri Gagarin, the first man to orbit the Earth— and the space race really took off.

OPPOSITE **In the 1800s, telescopes got bigger and bigger. When this 26-inch telescope was installed in the U.S. Naval Observatory in Washington, D.C., in 1873, it was the biggest refracting telescope in the world. Four years later, astronomer Asap Hall used it to discover the two moons of Mars, Phobos and Deimos.**

ABOVE **This U.S.-assembled German V-2 with an added upper stage, called the "Bumper," was the first missile launched at Cape Canaveral on July 24, 1950.**

Yuri Gagarin, the first man in space, on his way to launch. Gagarin's mission helped trigger the U.S.-USSR "space race." Behind him is a backup cosmonaut (that's what a Russian astronaut is called), who did not fly.

We owe most of what we learned about the planets and their moons in the last 60 years to this race. We started by investigating our own planet from space. The first U.S. satellite, Explorer 1, was launched on January 31, 1958, and it discovered that the Earth is surrounded by a vast, shifting belt of radiation that's kept in place by our planet's magnetic field. It was named the Van Allen Radiation Belt, after the American scientist who placed an instrument onboard Explorer 1 capable of detecting radiation. The cold war competition between the United States and the Soviet Union caused both sides to spend huge amounts of money developing new space technologies and training thousands of engineers and scientists. After Sputnik and Explorer 1, the main focus of the race was a competition to put humans on the Moon—which the United States did, triumphantly, in 1969. But while human spaceflight captured most of the attention, another very interesting thing was happening: robot space probes were being designed and built. At first, these mechanical explorers went to the Moon and took pictures in preparation for the human beings who would follow them. But soon they were being launched toward Venus, Mercury, and Mars—the *terrestrial*, or hard-surfaced, worlds of the inner Solar System—and then later out to the huge gas giant planets of the outer Solar System: Jupiter, Saturn, Uranus, and Neptune.

For the first time in history, we could send instruments —including sophisticated and powerful descendants of Galileo's telescope—to other worlds. Most of the pictures in this book come from such missions.

The two Voyager spacecraft, launched in 1977, were the first to explore all four of the giant Outer Planets. Both remain operational, with Voyager 1 (below), the farthest manmade object from Earth, almost 10 billion miles away. The long boom on the right holds the camera system, while the one on the left contains the spacecraft's nuclear batteries.

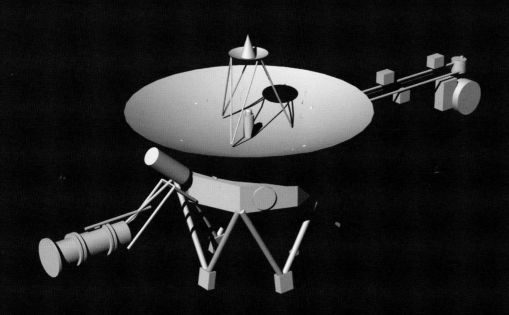

f you look at our planet from a certain angle—for example, from space—the name we've given it isn't very accurate. The Earth is actually covered mostly by water—lots of it. Seventy percent of our world's surface is ocean, so a better name for the third planet from the Sun might be "Oceana."

The Earth's oceans are where life started, and our world is still the only place where we know it has arisen. This doesn't mean it *is* the only place, of course; in fact, more and more planets are being discovered around other stars every year. And there are so many stars in the Universe that they're uncountable. So chances are that there are many solar systems where life has developed, and possibly millions or even billions of planets. If so, what does that life look like? Is it divided between plants and animals? Has it developed intelligence? We simply don't know. And the possibility remains that the Earth is the *only* place where life has arisen.

OPPOSITE A view of planet Earth gives evidence of an environment under serious strain. Smoke hangs over the rain forests of South America as Brazilian farmers use fire to clear land for agriculture at a rapid pace. On the horizon to the right, the entire west coast of Africa is visible. The third planet from the Sun, Earth has a circumference of 24,880 miles and completes an orbit around the Sun once every 365.2 days. MESSENGER, August 2, 2005.

Desert sand blows into the Atlantic
from southern Africa. OrbView 2,
August 18, 1999.

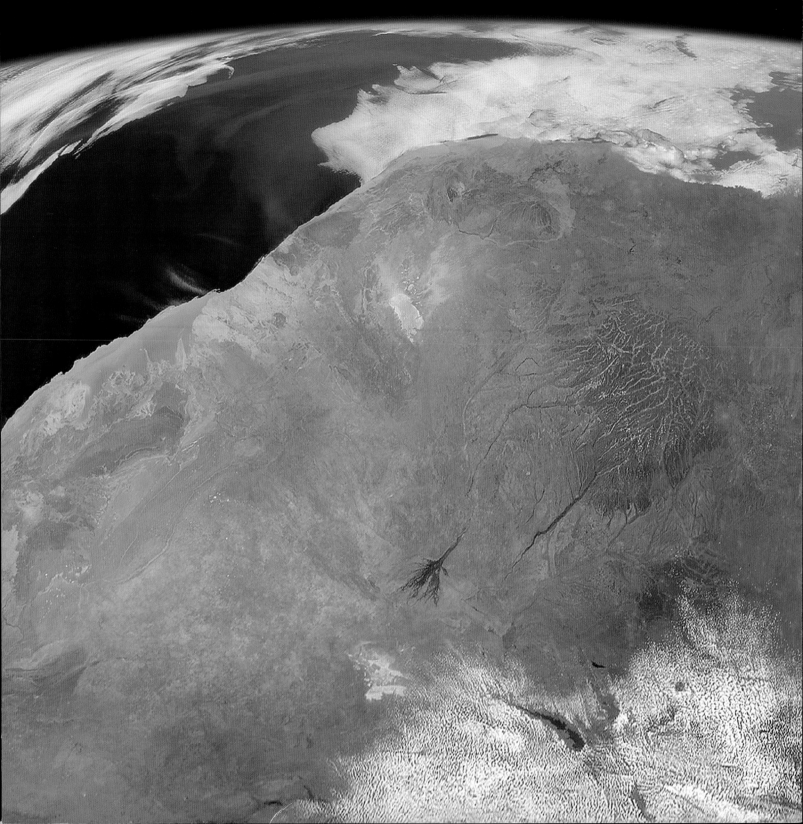

Our world is the largest of the terrestrial planets. However, it took the first photographs of Earth from space, in particular those from the Moon, to give us a powerfully strong visual sense of how tiny our planet is. Those photographs were incredibly important in the history of the human race. Apart from giving a sense of the true dimensions of our home, these extraterrestrial pictures showed us how fragile, beautiful, and borderless our globe is. From space, all the national boundaries we see on maps vanish, with only those that are coastlines remaining. The Earth is seen as it truly is: as oceans, seas, land, and polar ice, with huge banks of white clouds draped and scattered over everything. Also, everything looks flat on maps, but the true curvature of our world's surface is obvious from space.

Although the Earth was the first place ever photographed from space, the Moon was close behind. The first very blurry picture of the Earth from orbit was taken by the American Explorer 6 satellite in August 1959, and the first images of the far side of the Moon were taken by the Soviet Luna III probe only two months later. Because it always has the same face oriented toward Earth, the Moon's far side was completely unknown until then. Luna III was the first space probe ever to take pictures of another world and transmit them back to Earth.

A decision had been made to land astronauts on the Moon, and in the mid-1960s, NASA decided it was first necessary to produce a complete photographic survey of our nearest neighbor in space. To do so, the space agency

designed one of the most successful early space probes, called the Lunar Orbiters. Some of the photographs of the Moon reproduced here come from these missions. One of them, taken in 1967, shows the Moon and the Earth as two distinct worlds together in space. It is the first such photo ever taken. Only two years later, in 1969, U.S. astronauts Neil Armstrong and Buzz Aldrin landed on the Moon. It's still the only place in outer space ever visited by human beings rather than robot explorers.

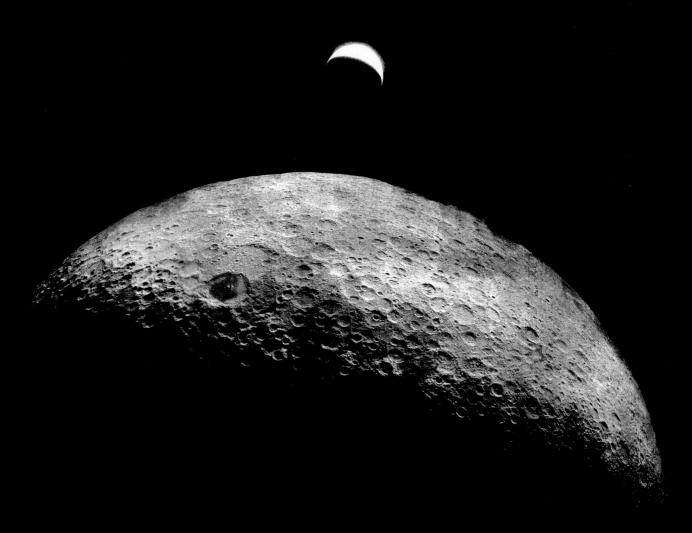

ABOVE **The far side of the Moon
and distant crescent Earth—the
first complete picture of both
worlds ever taken. Lunar Orbiter 2,
May 19, 1967.**

OPPOSITE **The Moon's massive
multi-ringed Mare Orientale impact
structure, which was formed by a
massive impact with an asteroid.
It is about 560 miles in diameter,
and its outermost ring, defined by
the Cordillera Mountains, is 3.5
miles high in places—the highest
mountains on the Moon. Lunar
Orbiter 5, August 18, 1967.**

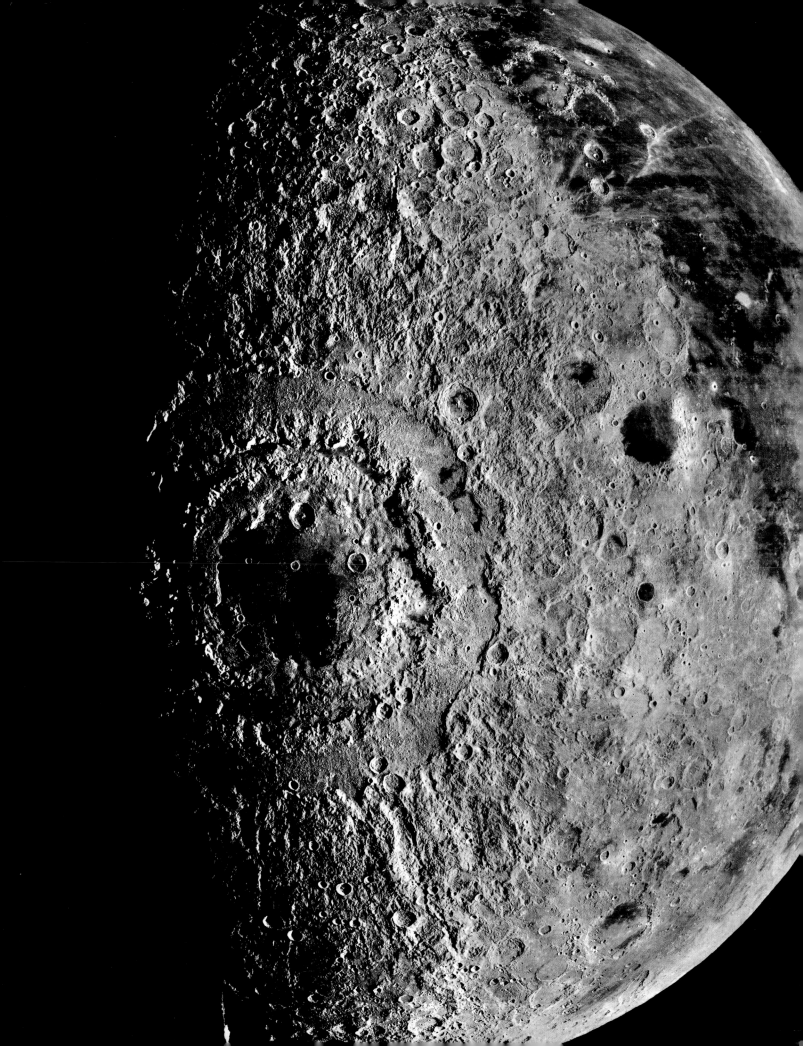

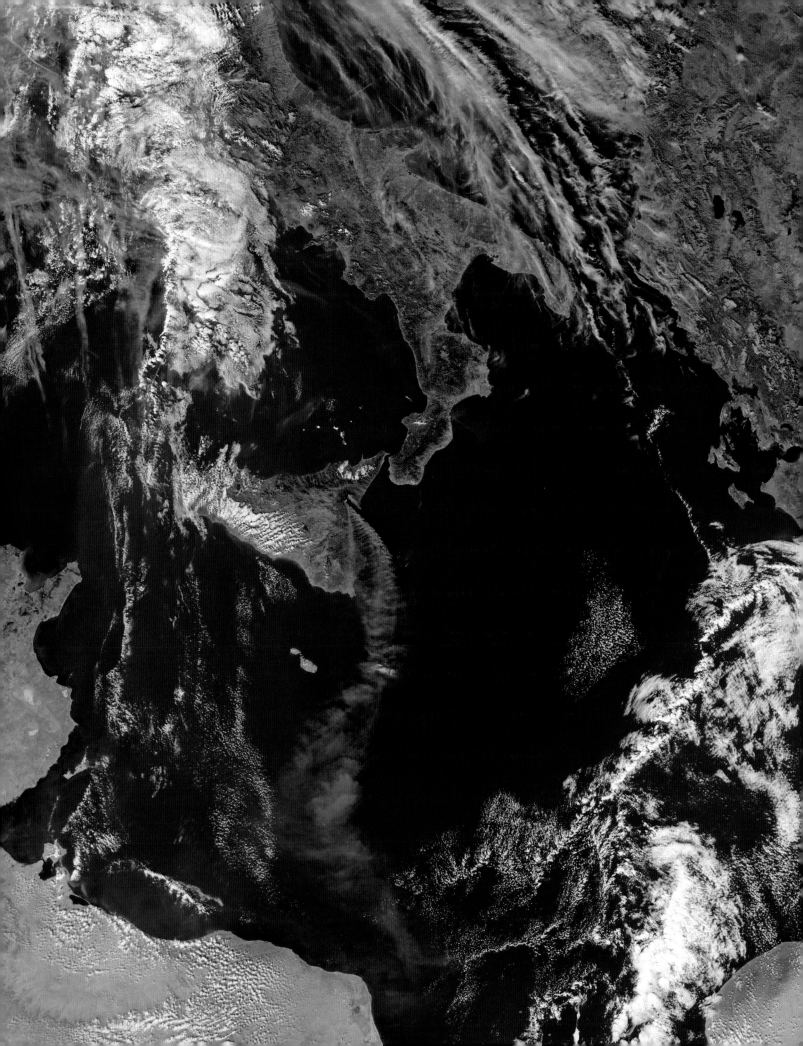

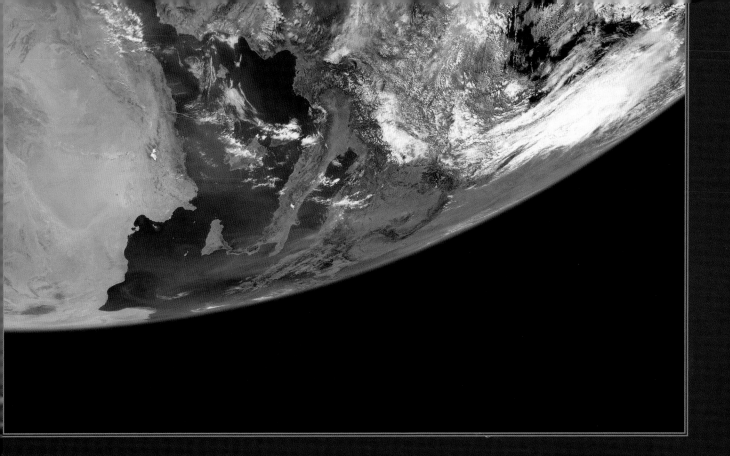

More than 20 years after the first pictures of the Earth and Moon together in space, another spacecraft was ordered to photograph our home world. Voyager 1, which had already flown past Jupiter and Saturn and was on its way out of the Solar System, was four billion miles away in 1990 when it was ordered to turn its cameras and face back toward the Sun and its planets.

As much as those earlier shots, Voyager 1's picture of a distant Earth gave us a new perspective on our place in the Universe. Far from being at its center, we had become something like a pale blue dot in a sunbeam. And yet, as the famous astronomer and space science advocate Carl Sagan also pointed out, that tiny point of light floating in deep space is where all of our history has taken place, where all of our leaders have come and gone, and where all known life has evolved over billions of years.

OPPOSITE **Sicily's Mt. Etna volcano erupting (near the "toe" of Italy's "boot"). To the right of Italy, Albania and part of Greece are visible. Aqua, October 30, 2002.**

ABOVE **Dust from the Sahara Desert blows toward Italy in this spectacular view of the Mediterranean Sea. OrbView 2, August 22, 2000.**

ABOVE **The Earth and Moon.
Galileo, December 16, 1992.**

BELOW **The Earth appears as a
"pale blue dot" in a beam of sunlight
in this image taken from four billion
miles away, at the edge of the Solar
System. Voyager 1, February 14,
1990.**

OPPOSITE Venus perpetually hides its face from the rest of the Solar System. The second planet from the Sun, Venus has a circumference of 23,627 miles and completes an orbit around the Sun once every 583.9 days. In this image, taken using ultraviolet light, cloud patterns that would otherwise be invisible can be clearly seen. Mariner 10, February 5, 1974.

C loud-covered Venus, the second planet from the Sun, is almost the same size as the Earth. In fact, due to its size and dense atmosphere, for many years Venus was considered to be our sister world. Because we had no way of looking through those clouds and because they reminded us of our own cloudy sphere, there was a lot of speculation about Venus. Could it have jungle-covered continents, perhaps with seas washing up against them, like Earth? Our uncertainty about the last point was so great that when the Soviets designed their first Venus lander, in 1961, they put a device called an accelerometer onboard, specifically to help scientists back on Earth see if it had landed on water. (Like many early robot space missions, this one failed before even leaving Earth's orbit in 1962.)

Not until the first successful interplanetary mission was the hope shattered that Venus might have water

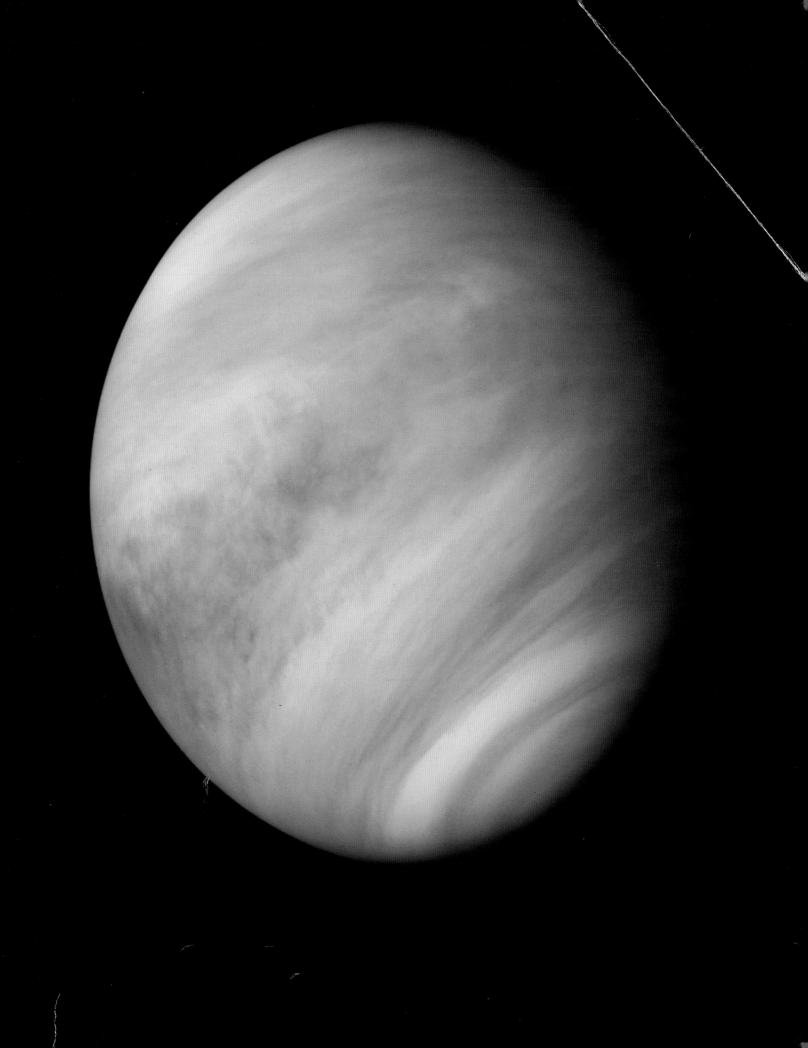

and possibly even life. In December 1962, the American Mariner 2 spacecraft flew past Venus at a distance of 21,644 miles. Its instruments revealed the surface to be extremely hot—far too hot for any known life. Later missions observed Venus to be hotter still—about 900° Fahrenheit, or about twice as hot as a standard kitchen oven can get, meaning hot enough to melt lead. The planet's extreme surface temperature is due to its clouds, which trap the Sun's light, making Venus by far the hottest place in the Solar System. Because Venus has a very small tilt in its axis of rotation, it has no real seasonal variation in temperature: it's simply baking all the time.

Speaking of seasons, not all planets have them, while some moons do. Those that do experience seasons have them for reasons as different as their changing distance from the Sun to the tilt of their axis of rotation, as on Earth. For example, Mercury has seasonal variations due to its changing distance from the Sun. Saturn tilts significantly on its axis, and its winter hemisphere—the one tilted away from the Sun—tends to turn blue, while its summer hemisphere is yellow. And one of Neptune's moons, Triton, has seasons because of Neptune's unusual orbit, which varies in its distance from the Sun by 62 million miles.

Venus was also revealed to have an atmosphere so thick and heavy that the intense atmospheric pressure at ground level is similar to the intense pressure of water half a mile below the surface of one of our oceans. We discovered this partly because early Soviet attempts to land robot probes

ABOVE The surface of Venus, a furnace of 900° Fahrenheit, as photographed by one of the 10 Soviet spacecraft to land successfully there. The spacecraft itself is visible at the bottom of this view reprocessed by Don P. Mitchell. Venera 13, March 1, 1982.

OPPOSITE Venus has a complex landscape marked by volcanic activity, mountain ranges, and asteroid impact craters such as the one visible at the upper center of this image. Radar image. Magellan, September 15, 1990–September 14, 1992.

on Venus used parachutes that were too large. Because of the density, or thickness, of the atmosphere, which is mostly made of carbon dioxide, the probes took so long to reach the surface that their batteries ran out of power before landing. Later, more successful Soviet landers used much smaller parachutes, so they could drift down much more quickly.

Until recently, Venus had been visited by more space probes than any other planet—18 Soviet and 6 American spacecraft. (Mars has now been visited by more.) The first landing on Venus—and on any planet in the Solar System—was accomplished by the Soviet Venera 7 probe in late 1970. By December 1978, an astonishing 10 Soviet and American spacecraft were to be found working on or above our closest planetary neighbor. Although a number of the Soviet landers sent back pictures of the Venusian surface, the only way to get a real sense of what the planet looks like on a larger scale is through radar images. That's because radar, which uses electromagnetic radiation instead of light to take pictures, can penetrate clouds.

In 1989, the U.S. Space Shuttle Atlantis launched a radar-mapping spacecraft called Magellan toward Venus. Arriving a year later, it spent two years using its dish antenna to collect data. What resulted was one of the most accurate maps of any planetary surface ever created. As it turns out, despite Venus's extreme conditions, it's a strangely beautiful place. Magellan's pictures revealed a mysterious world of volcanoes, lava flows, craters, and ridges. Venus has clearly been formed largely by volcanic processes.

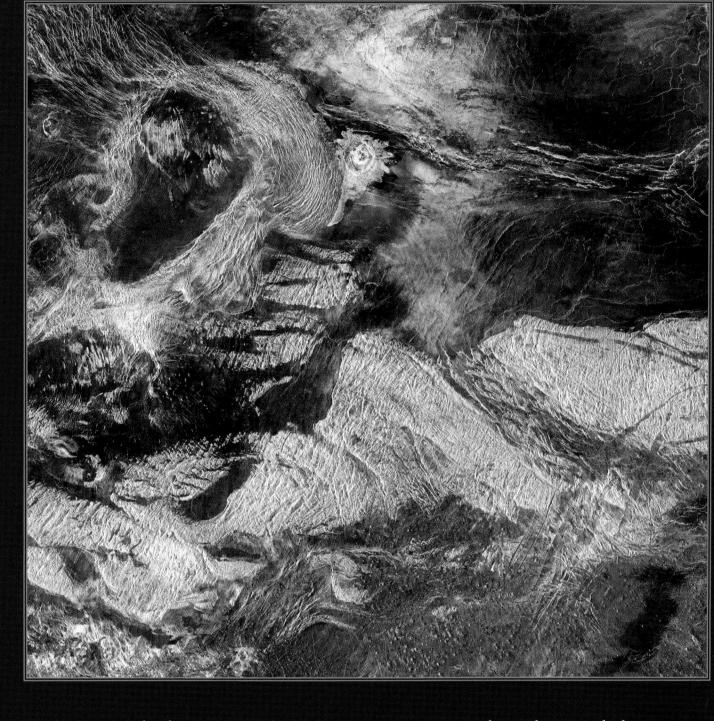

More recently, the European Space Agency sent a space probe to the second planet from the Sun. After arriving in April 2006, Venus Express set about producing the first temperature map of the planet's southern hemisphere, and it also provided evidence for past oceans on Venus. By late 2007 the spacecraft had confirmed the presence of lightning on the planet—and that it's more common there than on Earth! Clearly, this cloudy world still contains many surprises.

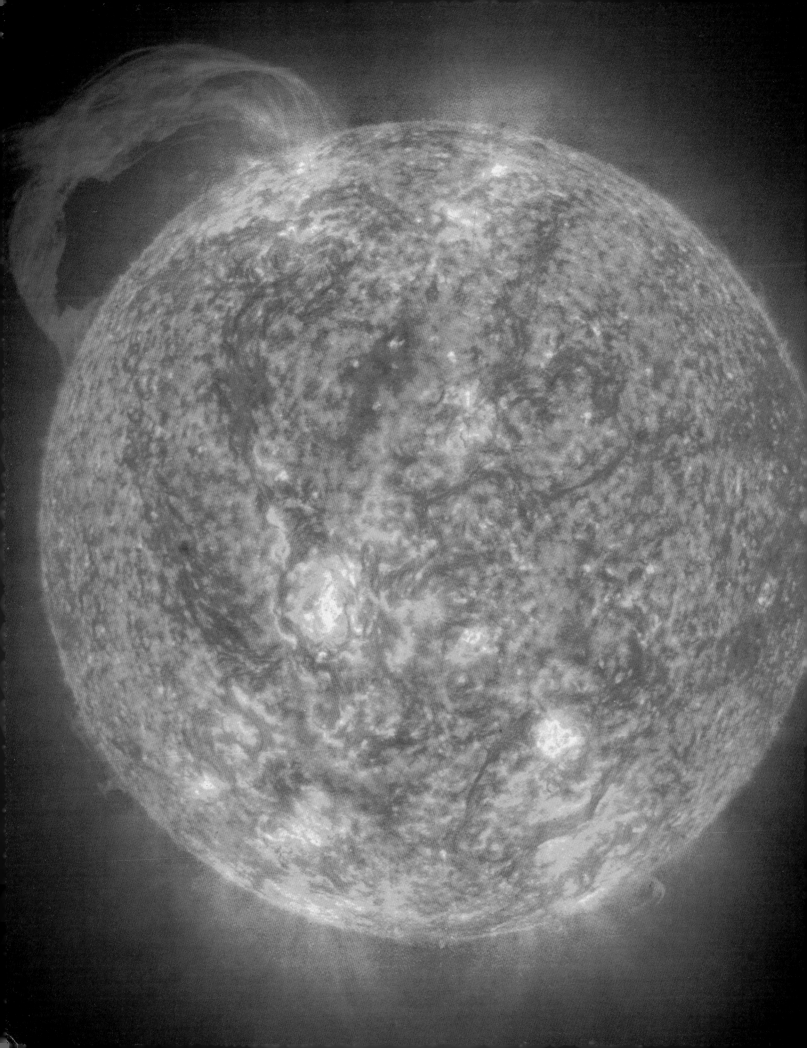

CHAPTER 4

THE SUN

There are no shadows on the Sun. Power rages and roars there relentlessly—a nonstop blast of raw heat and light flaring outward in all directions. This 4.6-billion-year-old ball of energy visible during the day from Earth is actually a star.

The Sun is so huge that it makes up 99.8 percent of the mass of the entire Solar System. (Remember, space itself is almost completely empty; it doesn't have mass like the Sun, the planets, and all the other objects in the Milky Way and other galaxies.) The remaining 0.2 percent—meaning every single planet, moon, asteroid, and comet in our Solar System—rotates around our central star. (True, moons rotate around their parent planets. But all the planets revolve around the Sun, with their moons in tow.) To consider the size of the Sun, whose radius is 109 times that of the Earth, is to realize how truly tiny we are. And the Sun is actually a very small component of our

OPPOSITE A massive eruption of solar material extends tens of thousands of miles above the Sun's surface. By far the largest object in the Solar System, the Sun has a circumference of about 2,713,406 miles—more than 100 times bigger than Earth. It completes an orbit around the center of the Milky Way Galaxy once every 225 to 250 million years. Ultraviolet image. SOHO, June 8, 2002.

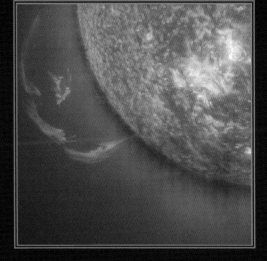

home galaxy, the Milky Way—just one of its uncountable billions of stars. Finally, the Milky Way itself is just one galaxy among billions of others in the Universe.

The star at the center of our Solar System is so powerful that it makes its influence felt even at night. Moonlight is actually sunlight, reflected off our closest companion world. We see the planets, too, because they're lit by the Sun.

The Sun belongs to a class of stars that scientists call "G2." There are about 100 million such stars in the Galaxy. This might sound like a lot, but our Sun is actually one of a limited class of stars. Astronomers have realized that the Sun and the rest of the G2 stars are, in fact, brighter than 85 percent of the other stars in the Galaxy. That's because most of the Milky Way is made of "red dwarfs." As their name indicates, these stars are less than half the size of the Sun, and they shine with a far dimmer, redder light.

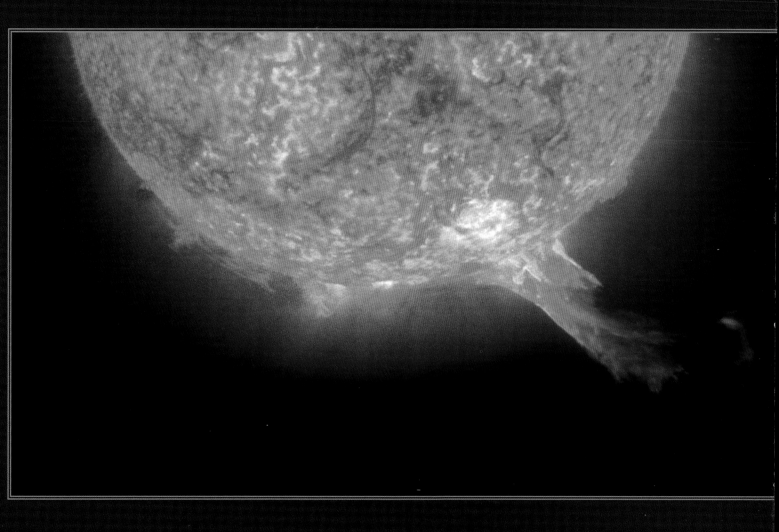

But how could the Sun be a star? Aren't stars those faint pinpoints of light visible in the sky at night, while the blindingly bright object we see during the day couldn't be more different? The answer is that the Sun is the only star near enough for us to experience it the way we do.

Because it is so close, the Sun is the only star we can study in detail. It shines as the result of a process known as nuclear fusion. Essentially, it is a spherical nuclear explosion kept from expanding beyond its current size because its immense gravity field exactly matches its outwardly directed power. In other words, the mass and gravity of the Sun is pulling inward at the same time—and

OPPOSITE A solar flare, or violent explosion on the surface of the Sun. Ultraviolet image. TRACE, July 23, 2002.

ABOVE A gigantic solar eruption vaults off the surface of the Sun. Ultraviolet image. SOHO, July 1, 2002.

at the same strength—as its huge ongoing explosion blasts outward. Every second, more than four million metric tons of matter are converted into energy in the Sun's core— producing the powerful radiation that we see as bright light and feel as heat here on Earth, 93 million miles away. The surface of the Sun is approximately 10,000 degrees Fahrenheit; the core is more like 27 *million* degrees—a figure not easy to comprehend.

The Sun also has a very strong magnetic field. That shifting field produces many of the different effects that we group together and call "solar activity." These include the huge eruptions from its surface called solar flares, as well as the strange "cooling loops" of descending matter that follow such flares.

One Earth year of 365 days equals one complete rotation of our planet around the Sun. Yet the Sun also orbits, moving around the center of the Milky Way Galaxy once every 225 to 250 million years. Given its age, the Sun has only completed between 20 and 25 orbits since it coalesced from interstellar dust and gas and ignited to become a star. It has only completed $^1/_{1,250}$ of an orbit since the first human beings appeared on its tiny satellite, the Earth. So if the Sun's orbit around the Galaxy's center was represented by the second hand on a clock, it would mean that the entire history of human beings on Earth has amounted to less—far less—than one second.

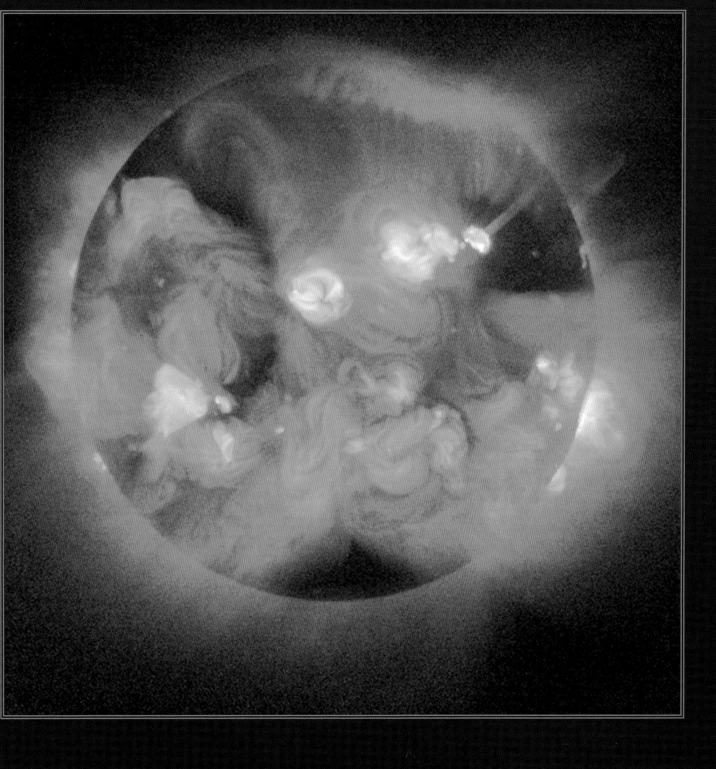

CHAPTER 5

MERCURY

OPPOSITE **Mercury (the small black dot at the horizon) in front of the Sun. The first planet from the Sun, Mercury has a circumference of 9,566 miles and completes an orbit around the Sun once every 87.9 days. TRACE, November 15, 1999.**

Mercury, the smallest planet in the Solar System and the closest to the Sun, is so small and near to our star that in photographs taken from on or near the Earth, it sometimes seems like it's on the verge of disappearing in a puff of smoke. (There's no danger of that, however; although close, the planet is far enough away to be safe from nuclear incineration.) Mercury's cratered surface and its lack of atmosphere gives it a similar appearance to our Moon, but it is 40 percent larger, though still less than half of our planet's size. It would take more than two and a half Mercurys to equal the diameter of Earth.

Although it actually didn't change at all, the innermost planet officially also became the smallest one in 2006, when distant Pluto was demoted from full planetary status by the International Astronomical Union. (Now considered a "dwarf planet," Pluto is only half the size of Mercury.)

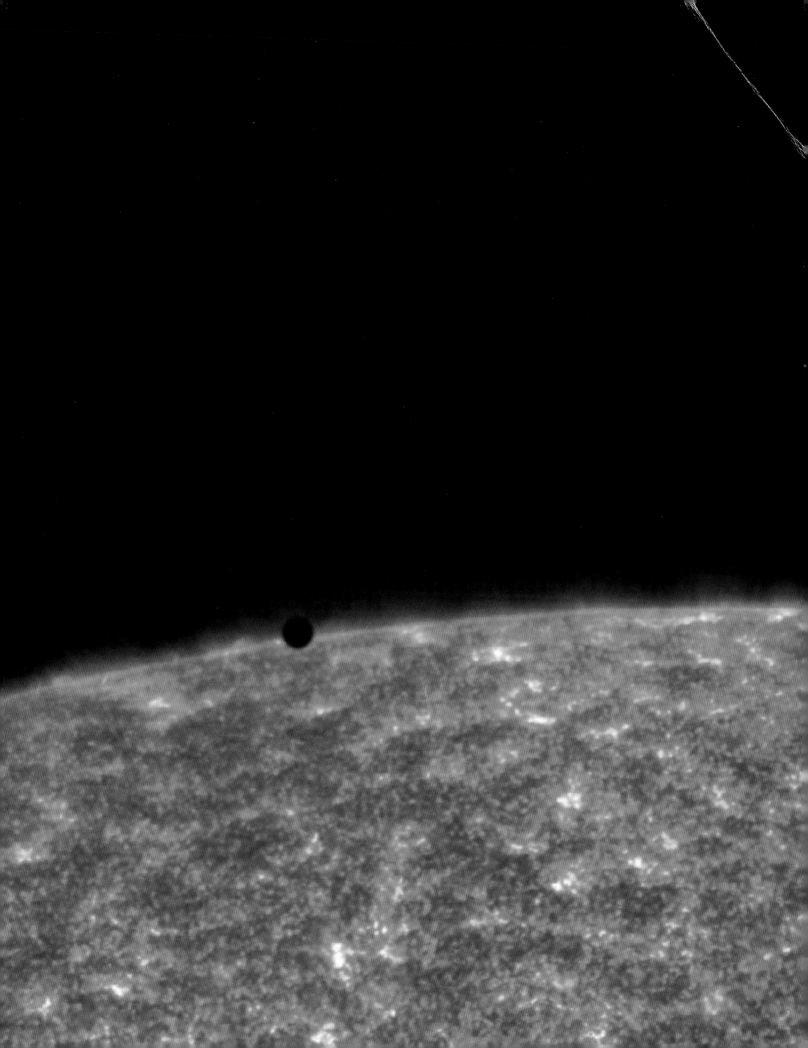

The closer to the Sun a planet orbits, the faster it moves, and Mercury is very fast indeed. Its year takes only 88 days, which is no doubt one reason why the planet has its name. Mercury is the Roman name of the Greek god Hermes, who invented fire and was in charge of bringing urgent messages down to mortal humans from the gods.

In fact, planet Mercury is so fast and so close to the Sun's dazzling rays that at first Greek astronomers believed it to be two planets—one visible only at sunset and one at sunrise. Mercury has a very eccentric orbit, meaning its distance from the Sun changes substantially. At its closest it's a scorching 28.5 million miles from the Sun; at its farthest, it's 43.5 million miles.

Although Mercury's year is short compared to ours, it has an extremely slow rotation rate, so its days are very long. Earth turns once every 24 hours, or 365 times per year, but Mercury only turns three times during two of its years, or once every 58 Earth days. This would produce some odd effects to anyone on its surface. From some locations, the Sun would rise and then increase in size as it climbed in the sky. When it reached its highest point, though, the Sun would seem to go *backward* for a while—heading back to the horizon from which it originally rose. But then it would reverse its direction yet again, now decreasing in size and eventually disappearing behind the opposite horizon from which it came. Meanwhile, the stars would move across the sky three times as fast as the Sun.

Mercury has only been visited by two robots from Earth. In 1974 Mariner 10 flew by and got the first close look at

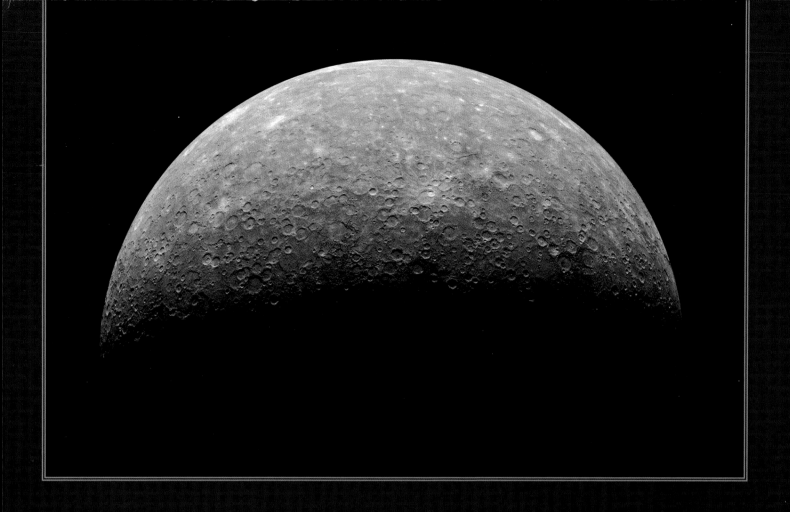

its surface, discovering the immense Caloris Basin, which is 963 miles in diameter. Very similar in appearance to the Moon's Mare Orientale, it came from the same cause: impact with a very large asteroid. The shock of that impact was so great that it created a ring of mountains more than a mile high on Mercury.

Mariner 10 only flew past the planet rather than orbiting it, so the space probe photographed less than half of Mercury's surface. In January 2008, a new probe called Messenger flew by the planet and photographed another 30 percent. This tiny robot will fly by two more times before it orbits Mercury in 2011. Bristling with seven miniaturized instruments designed to study the planet's thin atmosphere and cratered surface, Messenger will at first circle Mercury

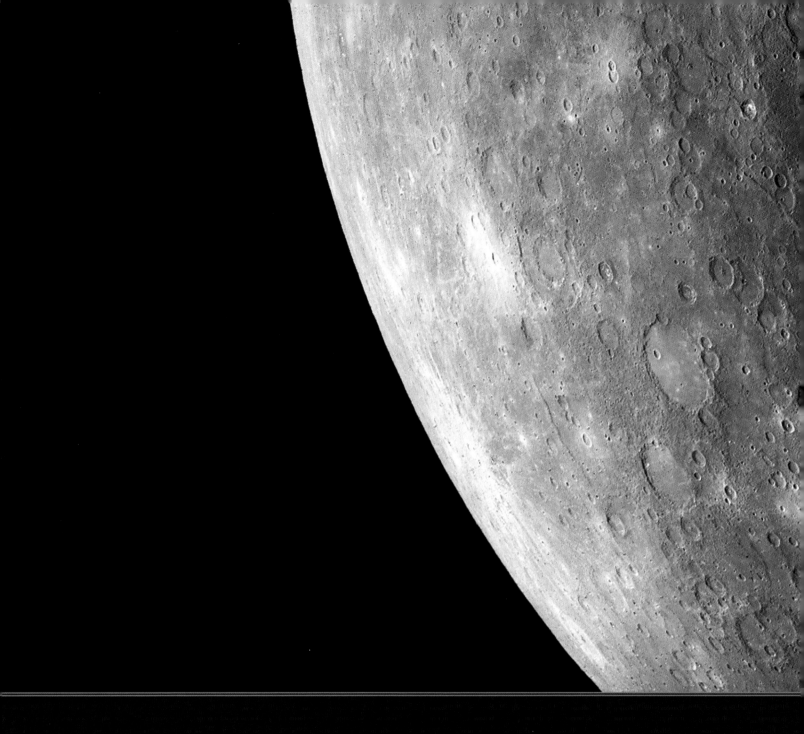

by imitating the planet's eccentric trajectory around the Sun. It will soar 9,400 miles over the planet's southern hemisphere before zooming down like an inquisitive gnat to an altitude of only 120 miles over the spectacular northern Caloris Basin. This orbit will gradually settle into a more circular path before Messenger conducts a thorough photographic survey of this hot and battered world.

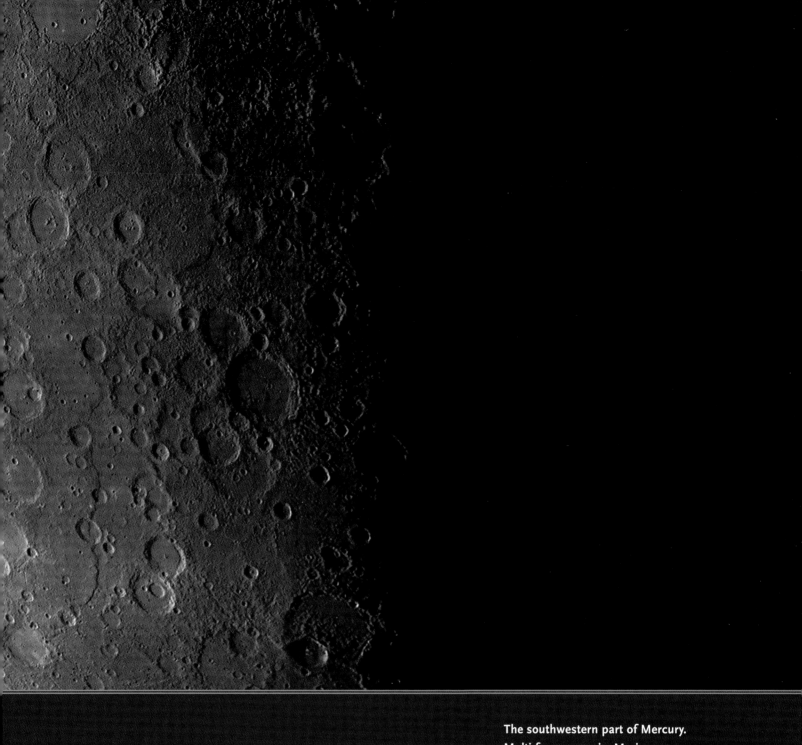

The southwestern part of Mercury.
Multi-frame mosaic. Mariner 10,
March 29, 1974.

CHAPTER 6

MARS

No other world has attracted more human interest than Mars, the third largest of the terrestrial planets and the fourth from the Sun. From the earliest days of human speculations about the lights wandering among the stars, Mars seemed somehow special. At first this was because of its color: the ancient Egyptians called it *Har decher,* meaning "The Red One." This bloody color also frequently associated the planet with war in the human imagination. Mars is named after the Roman god of war.

If the Red Planet looks a lot hotter than Venus, it's purely an illusion due to its color and its desert landscape. In fact, the temperature of the place averages a bone-chilling –81° Fahrenheit, and this drops far lower during the winter. Like Earth and some other planets, Mars has seasons caused by a tilt in its axis. In another reversal on Venus, the Red Planet's atmosphere is very thin. Mars is

OPPOSITE A full view of Mars with wispy clouds visible in the planet's thin atmosphere. At this time of year, the heavily cratered southern hemisphere is bathed in summer sunlight, which causes carbon dioxide and other gases to evaporate from the southern polar cap. This thickens the planet's atmosphere, and some of the gases migrate to the northern cap. The fourth planet from the Sun, Mars has a circumference of 13,300 miles and orbits once every 686.9 days. Rosetta, February 24, 2007.

red because its deserts are covered by a dusty powdered rust that comes from hematite, the mineral form of iron. These fine particles also fill the Martian sky, giving it a pink or orange appearance.

Mars has been the target of the most robot missions from Earth—and for good reasons. One is the possibility that life may exist there—or might have once. Another is that Mars is the planet most similar to the Earth in many ways, despite its temperature and atmosphere. As a result, at the time this book went to press, Mars had a total of six spacecraft working above or on its surface. Three were orbiting; two amazingly hardy rovers were still creeping methodically across its desert on opposite sides of the planet, four years after they landed; and a polar lander called Phoenix had settled in for a long stay.

With its thin atmosphere, how is chilly Mars like Earth? To begin with, it has polar ice caps, seasonal cycles, canyons, volcanoes, tornadoes, and global weather patterns. Its day is 24 hours and 39 minutes long—not so different from Earth's. And its landscapes look remarkably like those of the American Southwest, minus the Joshua trees. Mars also shows clear signs of once having had rivers and even oceans on its surface—though these are long gone. Its seasons are much longer, of course, because it takes the planet 687 Earth days to go around the Sun.

Mars is only half the size of Earth, so it has never been possible to observe it as well as we'd like to from home. But even as a fuzzy red blob in the lens of early telescopes, it was clear that the planet had polar ice caps and experienced

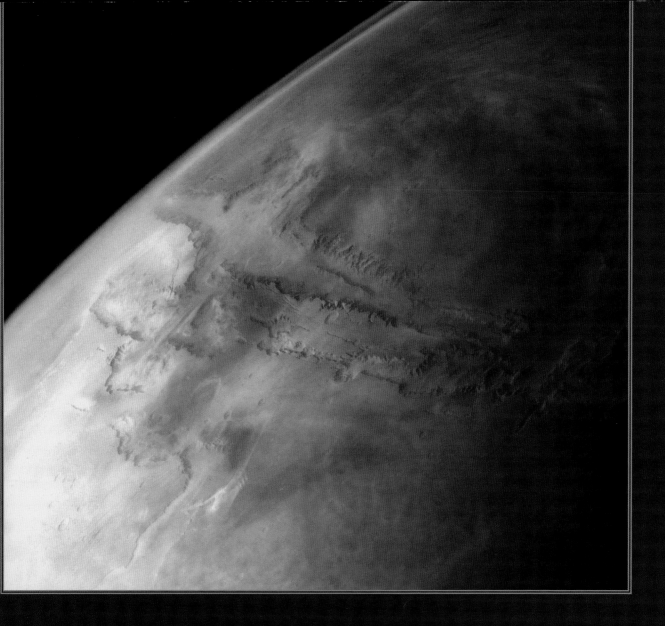

some seasonal surface changes. Astronomers struggling to interpret what they could see made a number of mistakes, however, and these only fueled our speculations about the place. For example, Mars's seasonal changes caused some observers to be convinced that there was plant life there.

And the mistakes didn't stop at speculations about plant life. When Italian astronomer Giovanni Schiaparelli turned his telescope in the direction of Mars in 1877, he thought he could see lines on the surface. He called them *canali*, or channels. In Italian, *canali* doesn't necessarily

ABOVE A view of the Valles
Marineris canyon system. Multi-
frame mosaic. Viking Orbiter 1,
August 17, 1976.

OPPOSITE Roughly 497 miles
long, Nanedi Valles may have been
formed in part by free-flowing
water. Mars Express, October 3,
2004.

suggest the work of intelligent creatures. These Martian features could have just been natural drainage channels. But when translated into English, they become "canals," which of course are made by intelligent beings. So the explanation behind these channels was literally lost in translation!

In the United States, amateur astronomer Percival Lowell was very influenced by Schiaparelli's writings. In 1894 he built an observatory in Flagstaff, Arizona, specifically to study Mars. Convinced that he saw a weblike network of canals there, he published a number of books about Mars that had a big effect on the public. Speculation grew that Schiaparelli's hard-to-see channels, which had become Lowell's canals, might be waterways built by an ancient Martian civilization. Their purpose, Lowell speculated, could be to bring water from the poles to the desert in order to irrigate crops.

As we now know, both Schiaparelli and Lowell were the victims of an optical illusion: they saw something that really wasn't there. Humans have a tendency to want to connect the dots to draw conclusions about something that we can't see very well. We now know that even the largest natural channels on Mars are far too small to be visible from Earth, even by the largest telescope. It's just that Schiaparelli thought that the illusion he was "seeing" was a natural phenomenon, and Lowell thought it was an artificial one. But the two astronomers' conclusions resulted in some very entertaining science fiction. Within a few years of Lowell's first book on Mars, English author H. G. Wells wrote one of the first (and still one of the most powerful) sci-fi novels, *The War of the Worlds*. In it, an ancient Martian civilization invades the Earth.

As bigger telescopes were built in the early 1900s, it seemed increasingly clear that canals don't exist on Mars. Certainly when Mariner 4, the first robot to visit the planet, flew by in 1965, there was no sign of them. Instead, Mars looked so cratered and inhospitable that its pictures were a shock to astronomers. It was only when later missions visited that it became clear that Mars's southern hemisphere (which was all Mariner 4 had time to photograph) has far more craters and looks much more like the Moon than its more Earth-like northern side.

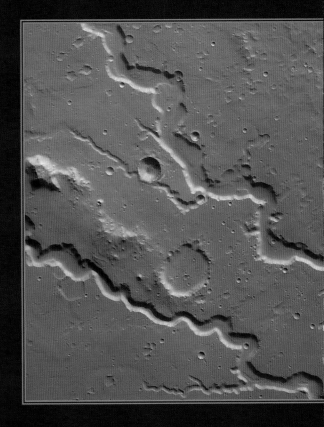

The Martian moon Phobos, the gray object to the right, hangs in space high above the 60-mile-wide Herschel Crater on Mars. Phobos itself is about 16.8 miles across. Viking Orbiter 1, September 26, 1977.

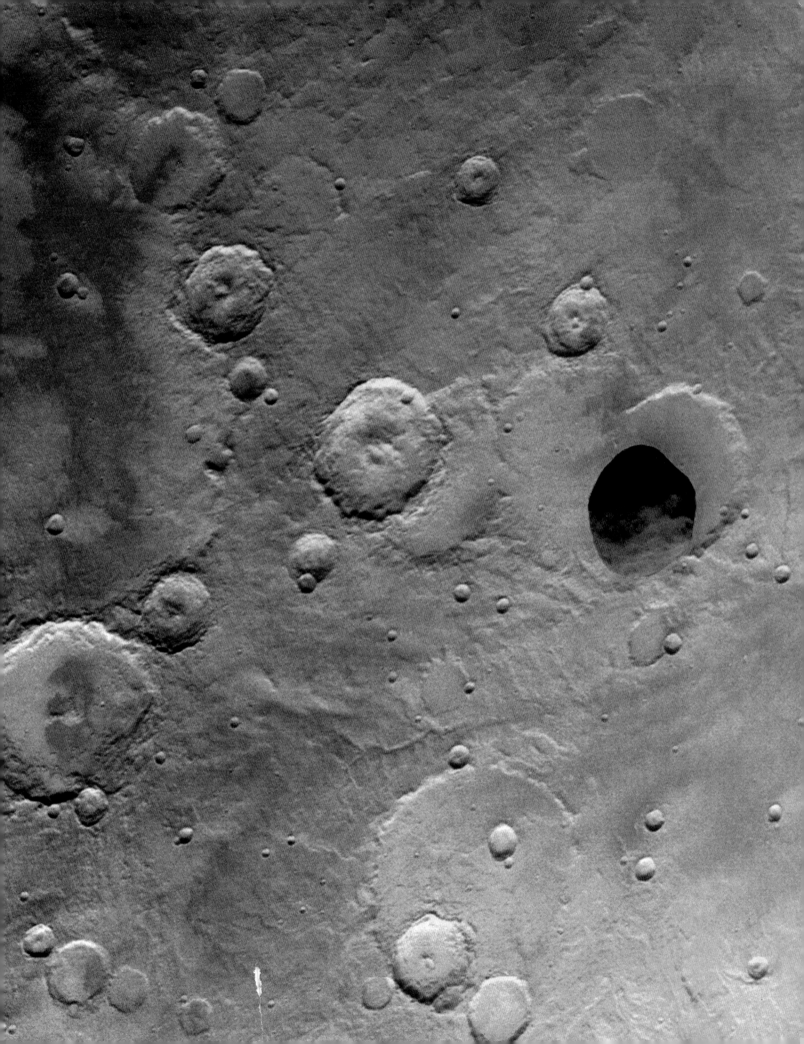

A global dust storm on Mars. Mars is the only planet known to have such all-encompassing storms, some of which last for months, transforming the planet into a featureless reddish-brown ball. Multi-frame mosaic. Viking Orbiter 2, February 19, 1977.

However, it took the arrival in late 1971 of the first probe to orbit around Mars to reveal the true fascination of the place. To begin with, Mariner 9 arrived in the middle of a planetwide dust storm. Mars, it seems, has enough of an atmosphere to allow for some pretty serious global weather. When the storm began to subside, observers on Earth at first saw a strange circular island poking out of the dust: the top of what eventually was revealed to be an immense, 16.7-mile-high volcano. (By comparison, the Earth's Mount Everest is slightly less than 5.5 miles high.) Now named Olympus Mons, it's the highest known mountain in the Solar System. (For a view of the 2-mile-deep crater at the top of Olympus Mons, see the front cover of this book, under the jacket.) And when the storm finally ended, the Mariner probe photographed a startlingly diverse landscape. The Martian terrain includes a giant, 2,500-mile-long canyon system later named Valles Marineris, in honor of its robotic discoverer. By far the

large quantities of liquid water on its surface, even if its surface is now bone-dry. So, in a sense, Schiaparelli had been proven right, almost a hundred years later—although none of those water channels are large enough to have been visible from Earth.

Mariner 9 put most of the remaining speculation about a onetime civilization on Mars to rest. But the evidence it presented of the past existence of liquid water on the Red Planet revived the idea that life of some kind may once have existed there, or might even still be hanging on.

In 1976, two of the most sophisticated devices ever to land on another world fired their retro-rockets and settled in for a long stay: the twin Viking Landers. After sending back panoramic views of the landscape, the landers

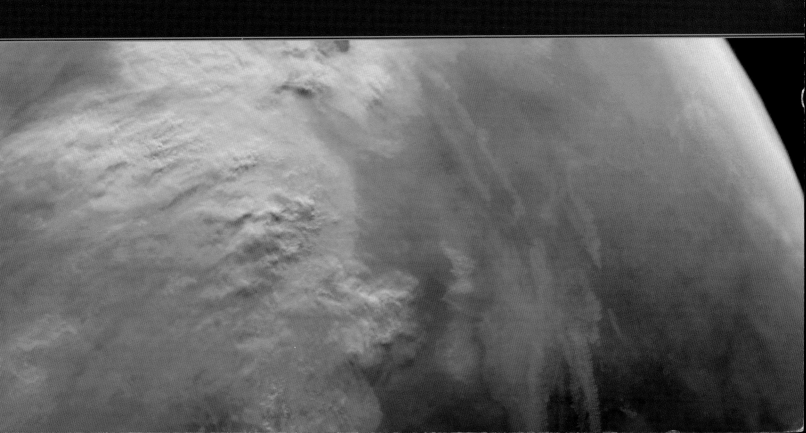

extended tubelike arms and picked up small amounts of soil. They then each conducted four different microbiology experiments. Although they were supposed to settle the question of whether or not life existed on Mars, these experiments didn't. The Viking results were generally accepted as negative, but they could simply have been based on material gathered in the wrong place. If there is life on Mars, it may well be hidden deep underground, where liquid water is thought to still exist.

Almost 30 years later, in January 2004, two of the most successful robots in the entire 50-year history of space exploration landed on Mars. Called Spirit and Opportunity, these six-wheeled, solar-powered rovers are the first vehicles capable of moving for many miles across the surface of another world. At the time this book went to press, they were both still operational, having lasted more than 17

times longer than expected. They've sent back a huge amount of information about the surface and atmosphere of Mars. They haven't discovered any evidence of life, but on the other hand, they weren't designed to.

In September 2009, another, far larger rover, the Mars Science Laboratory, should be launched to Mars. Four times as heavy and twice as wide as Spirit and Opportunity, this new rover is designed specifically to see if conditions suitable for life exist or ever existed on Mars. Like the Viking Landers, the new rover will carry an automated internal laboratory capable of analyzing soil samples. But the new lab-on-wheels will be much more sophisticated than the one carried by the Vikings, and, of course, it will be mobile. With luck, we should have a much better idea within a few short years of whether or not Mars ever could have supported life—and possibly even if it has life now.

OPPOSITE **Sunset on the
rim of Gusev Crater. Because of
ample dust high in the Martian
atmosphere, most of the sky is
pinkish orange; very fine particles
of dust are also responsible for
the blue glow that only appears
close to the Sun when it nears the
horizon. The result is a complete
reversal of the color scheme of
a typical sunset on Earth. Spirit
Rover, May 19, 2005.**

BELOW **Wispy clouds above cliffs
in the inner wall of Endurance
Crater on Mars. To the bottom
right, one of the rover's solar
power panels can be seen. Multi-
frame mosaic. Opportunity Rover,
November 13–20, 2004.**

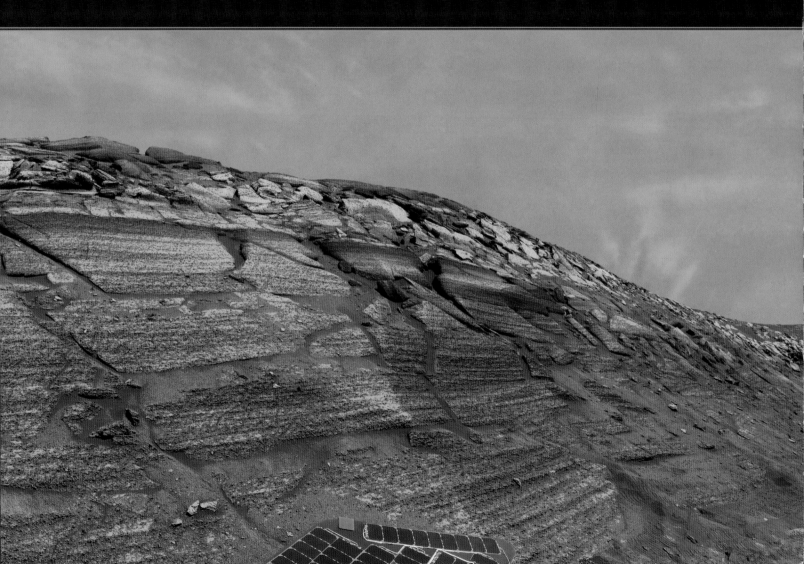

THE ASTEROIDS

According to the mathematically determined ratio of planetary distribution in our Solar System, there should be a fifth planet from the Sun orbiting between Mars and Jupiter—but there isn't. The absence of a planet in that zone was one of the unsolved mysteries of the skies in the late 18th century when the German astronomers Johann Titus and Johann Bode worked out the math of planetary distribution in 1772 and realized that a puzzling gap exists in that region. It wasn't until the first discovery of an asteroid, in 1801, that the missing-planet mystery began to be solved. That was when Giuseppi Piazzi, a priest who also taught mathematics in Sicily, Italy, spotted a small point of light apparently moving in an orbit outside that of Mars and inside that of Jupiter. (For a photo of Sicily from space see page 30.)

Piazzi's discovery led to many similar sightings, and soon the still widely accepted theory developed that a small planet or protoplanet—meaning a planet emerging from early Solar System gas, dust, and rocks (as all of the planets did)—had once existed in what we now call the asteroid belt. This object, or perhaps group of several objects, had most likely been destroyed by some force—possibly a collision between elements of the emerging planet—resulting in a vast ring of debris around the Sun. There was a Humpty-Dumpty quality to this smashup: the tumbling fragments that it produced couldn't ever come back together again because of the turbulent, shifting gravitational fields at play between Jupiter and Mars.

The attitudes of astronomers toward the thousands of dispersed fragments that are the Solar System's asteroids have ranged from fascination to scorn. Asteroids have been dismissed as the "vermin of the skies" (vermin being rats, cockroaches, and other unwanted creatures) and more reasonably referred to as "minor planets." But the word *asteroid* actually means "starlike object," which is clearly more of a tribute. While all three of these terms describing asteroids might seem exaggerated, the last one is actually the most accurate. This is because the materials that some asteroids consist of seem to have come directly from the explosion of early stars. We know this because most of the space rocks we call *meteorites* that fall to Earth are small fragments of asteroids. One of the two most common types of meteorite is made of the most primitive elements we know: silicates, iron, sulfides, and small beads of pure carbon (and sometimes tiny diamonds also). The chemical composition of such asteroids is approximately the same

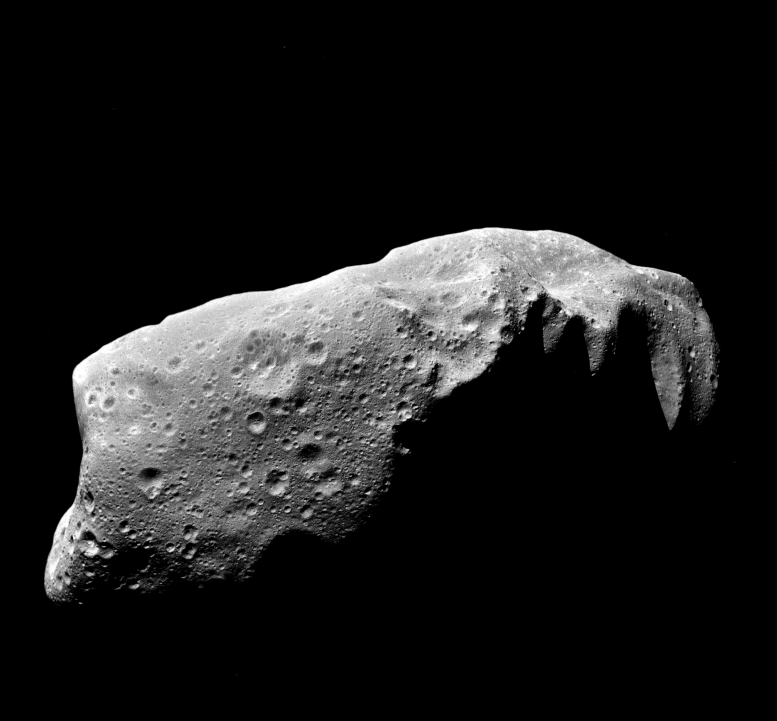

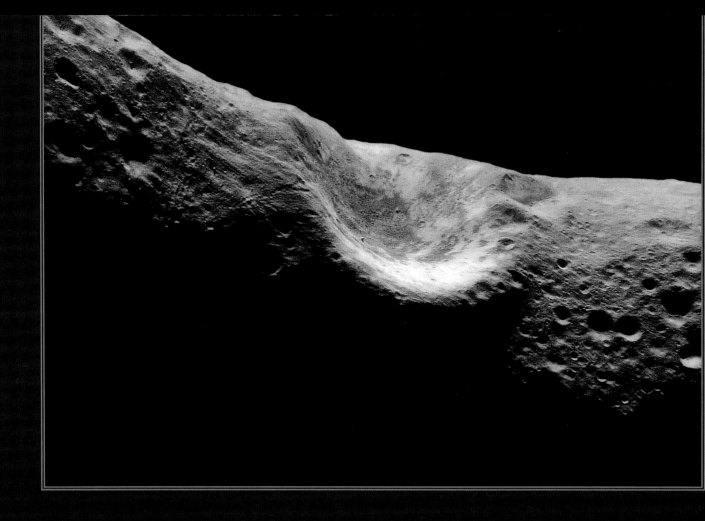

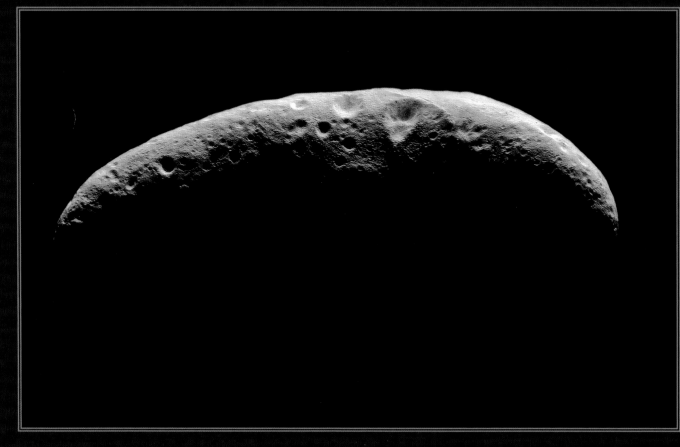

as the Sun as well as the primitive Solar Nebula—that disc of dust and gas from which the Solar System formed more than four billion years ago. According to scientists, the materials found in these meteorites indicate the elements that make up this most common type of asteroid were created *within* a star—with very little happening between then and now to disturb them.

The other kind of Earth-falling meteorite is different, however. It can contain solid iron, for example, or other metals such as nickel. Because these materials indicate the kind of natural separation of metals that can happen in a planetary crust, this kind of meteorite seems to have originated from inside a planet (or protoplanet) that once occupied an orbit between Mars and Jupiter.

Although Titus's theory and Piazzi's discovery seemed to indicate a single region where asteroids exist, the constant collisions among them within the asteroid belt spray lots of asteroids out into the larger Solar System. The Martian moon Phobos is thought to be a captured asteroid that perhaps originated in the belt, along with Mars's smaller sister moon, Deimos. (To see Phobos, turn to pages 60–61.) Theory has it that both moons were caught by Mars's gravitational pull. Jupiter also has a swarm of many small moons similar to asteroids, with 23 being discovered as recently as February 2003.

Some asteroids also cross the Earth's orbit—and these are by far the most dangerous to us. According to one widely accepted theory, the dinosaurs became extinct 65 million years ago after an asteroid estimated to be at least six miles

OPPOSITE ABOVE **Psyche, the largest crater on the asteroid Eros. Multi-frame mosaic. NEAR, September 10, 2000.**

OPPOSITE BELOW **A crescent view of the asteroid Eros. NEAR, March 31, 2000.**

BELOW **From some angles, asteroids can even resemble old tree trunks. NEAR, September 26, 2000.**

OPPOSITE **A crescent view of the asteroid Eros. Multi-frame mosaic. NEAR, September 8, 2000.**

wide hit the Earth with devastating effects. This danger clearly has not disappeared. Recent research indicates that many more asteroids have hit the Earth than we once thought (and also more recently than we thought). Partly due to the threat Earth-crossing asteroids pose, amateur astronomers have searched for and discovered many in the last decade or so. Thankfully, so far none appear to be on a collision course.

Starting in 1991, a handful of asteroids have been visited by robotic explorers from Earth. The first visit was by Jupiter-bound Galileo, which examined two asteroids, including 32-mile-long Ida, which turned out to have a small moon only about one mile wide. The first satellite of an asteroid ever seen, the moon was named Dactyl.

Two other missions have been specifically designed to visit asteroids: NEAR (for Near Earth Asteroid Rendezvous)

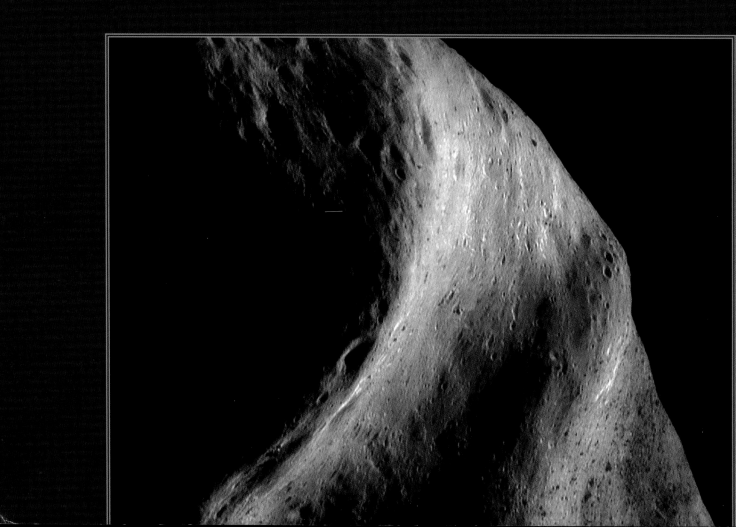

and the Japanese mission Hayabusa, or Falcon. The Japanese probe arrived at tiny Itokawa, an asteroid only about five football fields long, in late 2005. It discovered Itokawa to be a "rubble pile"—a loose collection of rocks and dust held together by their gravitational force. This is considered to be one common type of smaller asteroid.

Five years previously, in February 2000, the American NEAR probe entered into the orbit of another and far larger asteroid called Eros. The second largest of the 5,450 known near-Earth asteroids, Eros turned out to be 21 miles long. NEAR's camera revealed it to have an ancient, solid, cratered landscape. But the pictures accomplished something else: they showed that far from being "vermin," asteroids can be quite beautiful. After studying Eros for a year, NEAR was instructed to gradually lower its orbit. Finally, the spacecraft touched down on Eros's dusty, ancient surface. It was the first landing on an asteroid by a spacecraft from Earth.

CHAPTER 8

THE JUPITER SYSTEM

OPPOSITE **The fifth planet from the Sun, Jupiter is by far the biggest planet, with a circumference of 279,118 miles. It completes an orbit around the Sun once every 11.8 years. Cassini, December 29, 2000.**

Jupiter, the largest of all the planets, rules a complex, extended system of large moons, asteroid-like moonlets, and faint and tenuous rings. (All four of the giant outer planets have ring systems, but only one, Saturn, has significant rings that are visible by telescope from Earth.) Three of Jupiter's four large moons are icy and frozen, while the other is hot and fiery. Taken as a group, they are fascinating in their variety; taken individually, they're dazzling in their strangeness. The wheeling Jupiter system is a kind of Solar System in miniature. Its immense central planet is the first of the four planets known as "gas giants"—a big, bulging sphere of hydrogen and helium.

Jupiter is sometimes considered a kind of failed star, one that didn't quite manage to gather enough material from the protosolar nebula (the flat disc of rubble, gas, and dust out of which the Solar System formed about 4.6 billion years ago) to ignite. But Jupiter still radiates

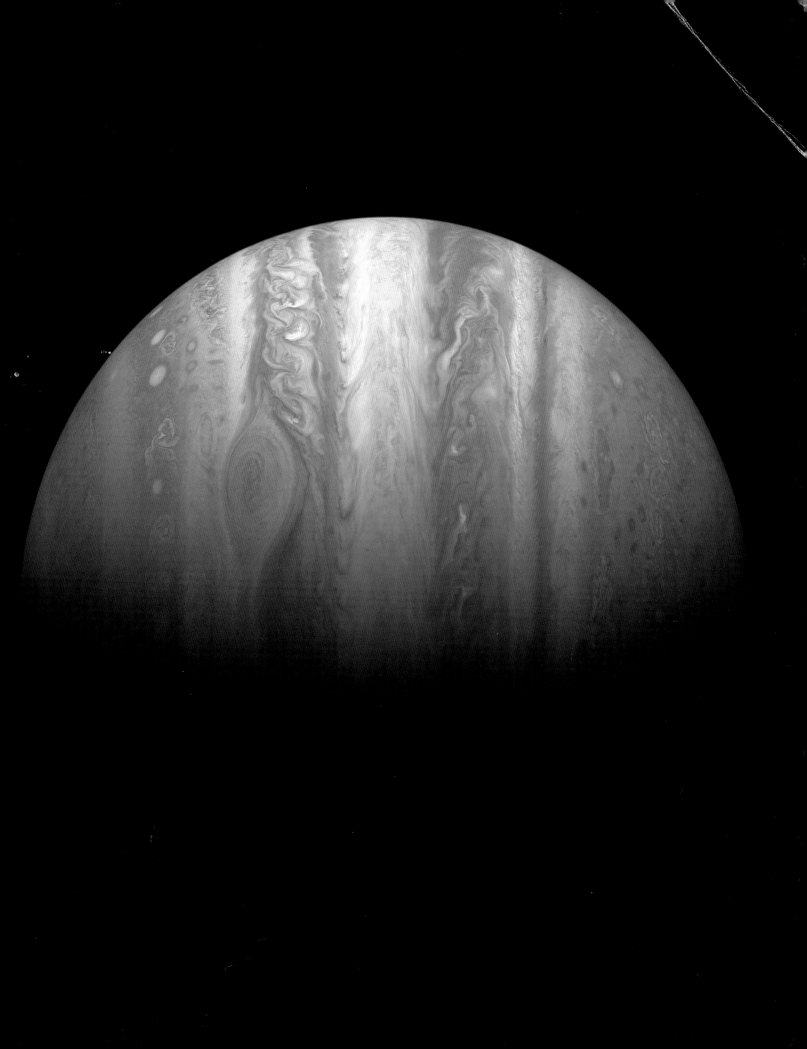

far more heat than it gets from the Sun. It didn't do so badly in the size department, either: this rapidly spinning banded ball is more than twice as massive as all the other planets combined. In fact, Jupiter is large enough to cause the Sun, 483 million miles distant, to wobble slightly from its gravitational pull. This wobble is how observers from distant solar systems might be able to determine that our star has at least one planet orbiting it. (This is one way we discover planets around other stars.) The fifth planet from the Sun, Jupiter occupies the Solar System's middle ground and has 63 known moons.

Although dwarfed by their giant master, two of Jupiter's four large moons are the size of terrestrial planets in their own right. Ganymede, one of the four discovered by Galileo in 1610, is the biggest moon in the Solar System and larger than the planet Mercury. Callisto, one of the most cratered objects known, is only slightly smaller. But the fire-and-ice pair of Io and Europa presents a bizarre spectacle. These two strange worlds, each about the size of our Moon, may be the two most fascinating deep-space objects yet observed.

Europa almost certainly contains a liquid water ocean under its fissured ice. By some estimates, Europa may contain more water than all of the Earth's oceans combined. Curving cracks on Europa's frozen face, some of which are linked in long chains, give clear evidence that its ocean isn't just wishful thinking. These linked cracks are thought by planetary scientists to have formed according to the pull of Jupiter's gravity. They are the result of the powerful, constantly shifting pressure exerted by liquid water under the ice, which is pulled toward the huge planet during each of Europa's orbits around Jupiter. Jumbled fields of icebergs in parts of the crust have apparently thawed and then been refrozen; they also indicate the presence of liquid water under the ice.

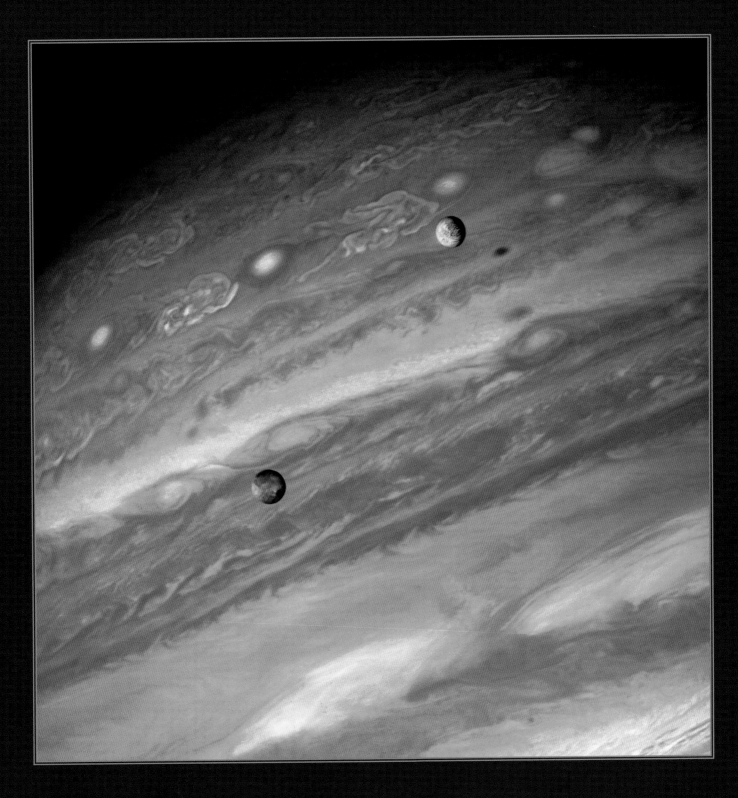

A closer view of Jupiter's spinning
Great Red Spot, a cyclone to end all
cyclones. To give a sense of scale:
the storm is larger than the entire
Earth from top to bottom and more
than twice as wide as our planet
from side to side. Voyager 1, March
3, 1979.

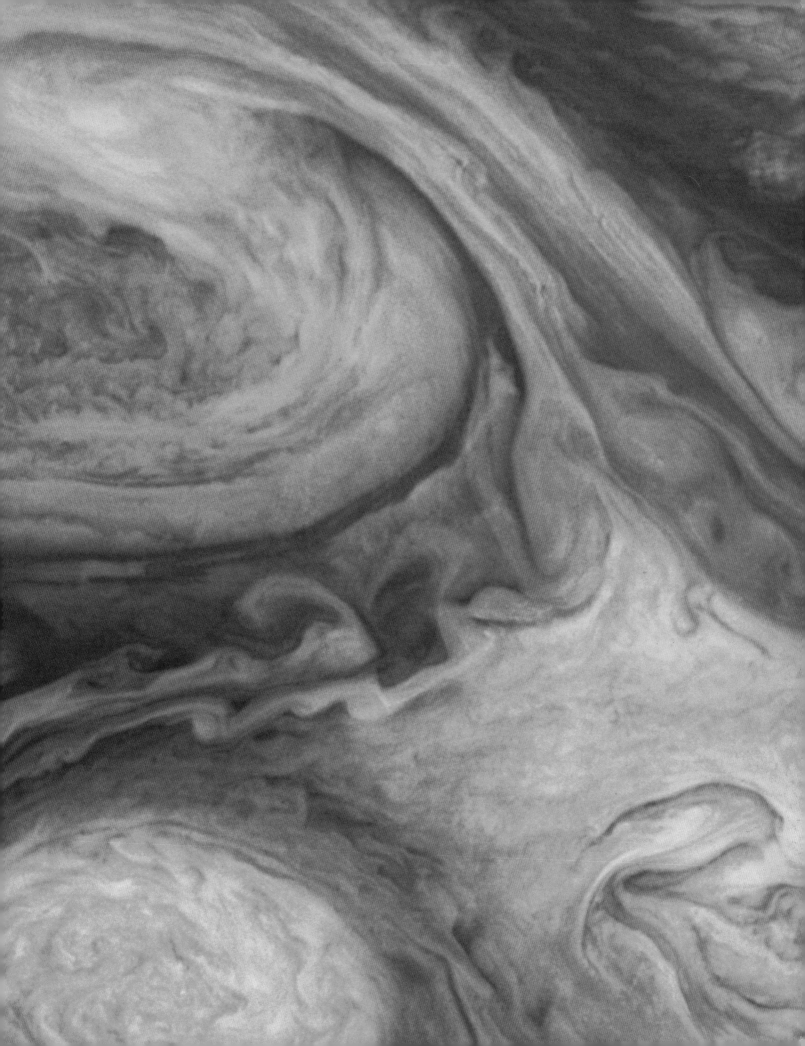

As a result, Europa now ranks along with Mars at the top of the list of potential homes for extraterrestrial life. After all, every known form of life requires liquid water.

By contrast with pale Europa, yellow-orange Io, Jupiter's innermost large moon, is the most garish place in the Solar System. More volcanic than any other known moon or planet, Io is squeezed by the gravitational pull of Jupiter and by the opposing pull of its three large sister moons. As a result, Io is constantly boiling inside. Lava is forced out from under Io's surface at high pressure, producing towering plumes of volcanic sulfur that blast more than 300 miles into space. Because this moon constantly replaces its outer surface with materials expelled from

OPPOSITE **Tens of thousands of cracks in the ice are visible on Jupiter's moon Europa. The moon almost certainly possesses a vast, ice-capped global ocean. Galileo, March 29, 1998.**

ABOVE **Europa, the ocean moon, in front of Jupiter's Great Red Spot. Multi-frame mosaic. Voyager 1, March 3, 1979.**

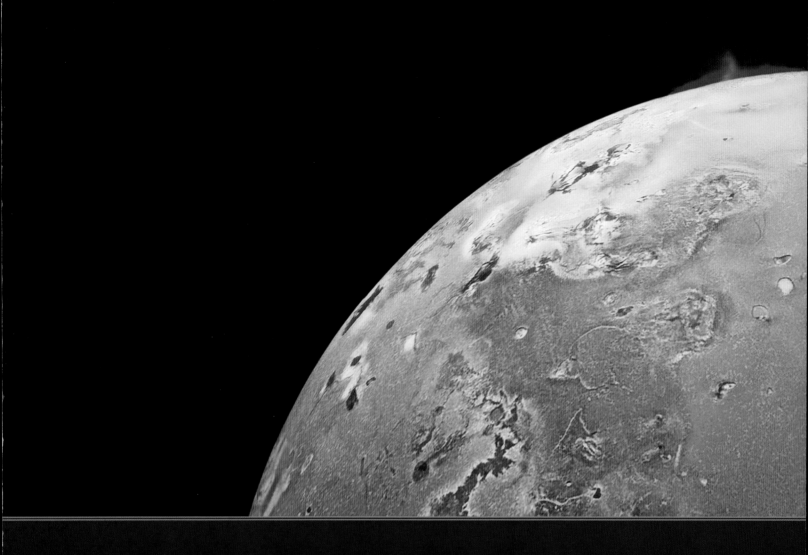

A volcanic eruption sends an 86-mile-high blue plume above Jupiter's moon Io. The volcano is named Pillan Patera, after a South American god of thunder, fire, and volcanoes. Galileo, June 28, 1997.

inside, Io has the youngest landscape of any Solar System object. Its various shades of yellow, orange, and red are thought to correspond to the temperature of the lava as it starts to cool.

The immense object at the center of this collection of strange moons is no less fascinating. Planet Jupiter is a raging ball of storms, cloud currents, and flickering lightning bolts. Because Jupiter spins more rapidly than any other planet, completing one rotation every 10 hours, its diameter is larger at its equator than it is at the planet's poles, due to the resulting centrifugal force. (Centrifugal force is a force that pulls a rotating or spinning object

away from the center of its spin.) And Jupiter's high rotation speed is also thought to be the reason why its atmosphere is "smeared" into different-colored bands of clouds. Below the clouds, which are mostly hydrogen, helium, and ammonia gas, there is thought to be a layer of liquid hydrogen. Below this level, gravity mashes Jupiter's dominant element into something called metallic hydrogen, which is a compressed form of the element. Deep down under all the hydrogen, a rocky core is thought to exist that's from 12 to 45 times the size of Earth. This core is so pressurized by the weight of everything above, it might contain huge diamonds!

Jupiter was named after the Roman king of the gods, and its first telescopic observers in the 17th century must have suddenly realized just how appropriate the name really was. Not only does this planet rule over many moons, it also has a single, glaring red eye, which must have seemed to stare angrily back across the Solar System at these first human observers. This, the Great Red Spot, is actually a vast storm system more than twice as large as Earth and at least 300 years old.

OPPOSITE **The volcanic landscape of Jupiter's moon Io. Io's startling color variations suggest that the lavas and sulfur deposits from its many active volcanoes are composed of complex mixtures. Galileo, July 3, 1999.**

BELOW **Io high above Jupiter's cloud-tops. The image is deceiving: There are 217,480 miles, or roughly two and a half Jupiters, between Io and the planet's clouds. Cassini, January 1, 2001.**

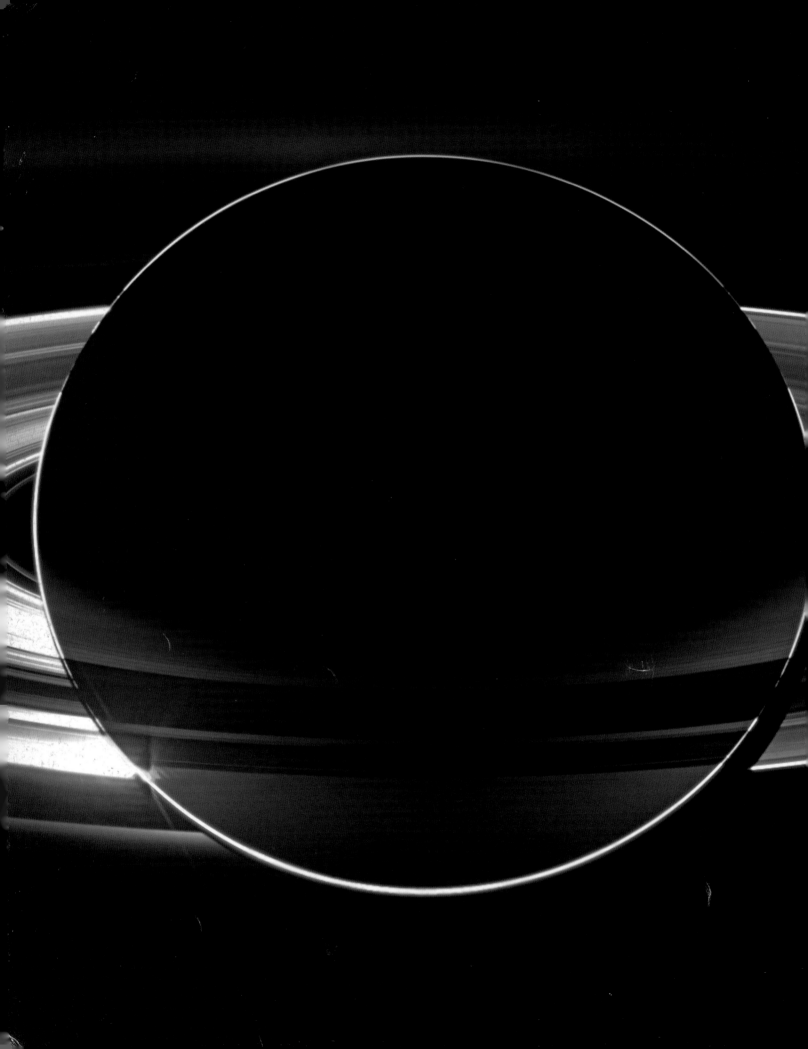

SATURN

When Galileo first pointed his telescope at Saturn back in 1610, he was truly confused for the first time since he'd started using the instrument during the previous year. His earlier observations were remarkable, but they weren't that hard to understand. Mountains on the moon? Surprising, yes—at least to its first observers—but we have mountains here on Earth. A Venus that goes through phases, transforming itself over a period of weeks from crescent to full disc? Interesting—but we've seen our Moon do that for many thousands of years. Satellites orbiting Jupiter? Fabulous, but we have one ourselves.

In the case of Saturn, though, here was a world with—what? Handles? Ears? Two equally large moons, spaced on opposite sides of the planet? All of these were ideas, however unlikely, that Galileo considered to try to explain the rings. And to make things even more puzzling, within a couple years these two strange, symmetrical objects had

OPPOSITE **Sunset on Saturn. The indirect light on the rings provides a view never before seen, with previously unknown faint rings illuminated. The second-largest planet, and the sixth from the Sun, Saturn has a circumference of about 235,298 miles and completes an orbit around the Sun once every 29.6 years. Cassini, September 15, 2006.**

BELOW **Early in 2007, the Cassini Orbiter shifted its orbit to climb high above the plane of the rings. This spectacular view is from above the planet's north pole. Cassini, January 20, 2007.**

OPPOSITE **Saturn's moon Mimas is seen against the cool, blue-streaked backdrop of Saturn's northern hemisphere. Shadows cast by the rings arc across the planet, fading into the darkness on Saturn's night side. Cassini, November 7, 2004.**

vanished entirely. "I do not know what to say in a case so surprising," Galileo wrote to a friend in 1612. Although he clearly didn't realize it, he had become the first astronomer to witness a Saturn "ring-plane crossing," which occurs approximately every 15 years, when the sixth planet tilts in such a way that its incredibly thin rings are edge-on to the Earth, making them appear to vanish for a while.

Galileo had an excellent imagination of course, but his telescope could magnify only to the 20th power—making it about twice as strong as a regular pair of binoculars. And Saturn's tilt in the years when he observed it didn't make its rings any easier to understand. It wasn't until 1656 that Dutch astronomer Christiaan Huygens, equipped with a telescope more than twice as powerful as Galileo's that he'd designed himself, understood that the second-

largest planet is surrounded by "a thin flat ring, nowhere touching." By 1676 another Italian, Giovanni Cassini, had discovered the largest gap in the rings, which is now called the Cassini Division. From then on, Saturn had an A and a B Ring. (The other rings were given letter names in the order of their discovery.)

Saturn is probably more responsible than any other planet for changing ordinary Earthlings into astronomers. It's hard to look at it through a telescope for the first time without an amazed whistle. Similar in some ways to Jupiter, although calmer and smaller, Saturn is a gas giant, with an internal heat source and less-prominent clouds than Jupiter that are also made mostly of hydrogen.

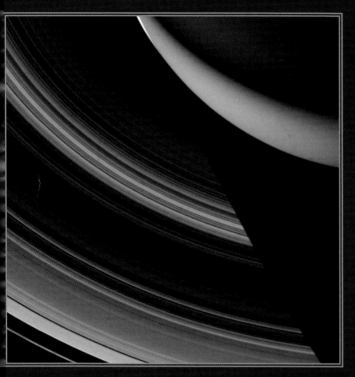

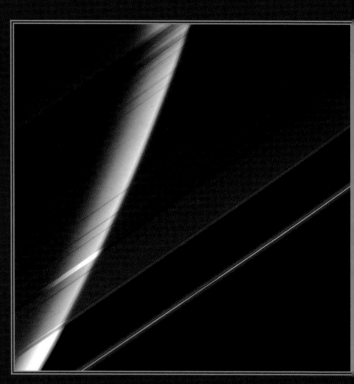

TOP LEFT Saturn's majestic C Ring arcs into view from the shadow of the planet. Cassini, December 15, 2006.

TOP RIGHT The planet's swirling atmosphere and rings are viewed from 700,000 miles above the planet's north pole. Cassini, October 30, 2006.

BOTTOM LEFT Almost all of Saturn's rings, sweeping into the shadow of the planet, are seen in this image. Cassini, December 5, 2006.

BOTTOM RIGHT One space within the ring, seen at the outer edge, is known as the Encke Division. Ice particles in the rings act as filters, allowing us to see haze in the planet's upper atmosphere. Cassini, November 4, 2006.

But Saturn's wheeling rings put it in another category altogether. It wasn't until the 1979 arrival of the first mission to Saturn, Pioneer 11, that the true complexity of those formations became apparent. Only a year later, the first of the two Voyager spacecraft, which passed Saturn in 1980 and 1981, discovered many more rings than had previously been suspected, with thousands of gaps and ringlets. The Voyagers also discovered two tiny moons within the F Ring—Prometheus and Pandora.

Although they may look solid from a distance, the rings are actually made of many tens of thousands of pieces of ice, with some rock and dust in the mix. The larger chunks are about the size of a car, and from there they descend in size to pebbles, gravel, sand, and smoke. Probably the remains of a moon that was shattered by a collision, the rings are extremely thin for their diameter. They are about 60 feet thick versus an astonishing 180,000 miles from edge to edge. This ratio is comparable to that of a very thin sheet of paper extending across an area as large as a football stadium.

The arrival of the Cassini Orbiter in 2004 after a seven-year flight from Earth has provided much new information about Saturn's rings and its 60 moons, most of which are quite small, as well as about the huge planet itself. The largest and most complex interplanetary probe ever built, Cassini carried another robot on its back. Called Huygens, this small European atmospheric-entry probe was designed to explore Titan, Saturn's largest moon. Entirely covered by dense brown clouds filled with organic chemicals, smoggy Titan is bigger than planet Mercury and is the only moon

BELOW This image is one of the first to show Saturn's moon Enceladus spewing water vapor and ice particles from its south pole. The background space is noticeably brighter than Enceladus's dark side due to particles in Saturn's E Ring, which the moon's geysers feed. Cassini, November 27, 2005.

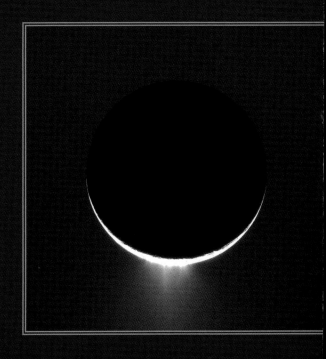

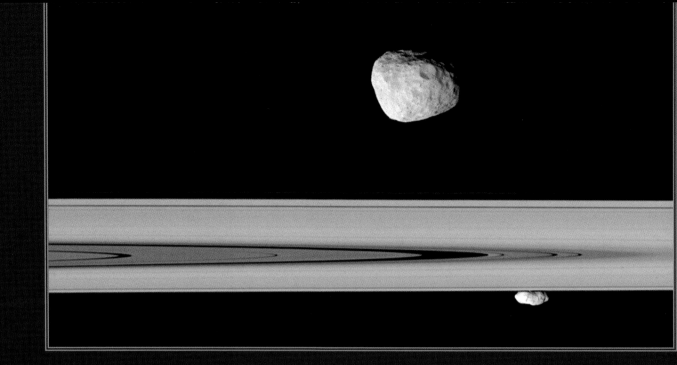

ABOVE Saturn's moons Janus (above) and Prometheus (below) look close enough to touch in this stunningly detailed view. From just beneath the rings, Cassini observes Janus (113 miles across) on the near side of the rings and Prometheus (63 miles across) on the far side. Cassini, April 29, 2006.

OPPOSITE Images taken from four different altitudes as the European Space Agency's Huygens probe descended toward the surface of Saturn's smoggy moon Titan under parachutes. Huygens, January 14, 2005.

with a thick atmosphere. It has long fascinated planetary scientists, in part because it is thought to resemble an extremely cold version of early Earth.

Huygens parachuted to Titan's surface on January 14, 2005, sending a flood of information during its slow descent and after it landed. Because it wasn't known if Titan had seas, Huygens was designed to float if it had to—though it landed on damp but solid ground. Still, Huygens's images made it clear that Titan's surface is defined by drainage channels, rivers, and lakes. Both wind and rain have lashed this dimly lit world. Although its weather has made it look surprisingly similar to parts of our planet, with a surface temperature of −288° Fahrenheit, Titan is far too cold for liquid water. Instead, its rivers, lakes, and seas are filled with fluid hydrocarbons like ethane and methane—substances that become gas at warmer temperatures, not unlike what gas stoves use.

Ever since its arrival, Cassini has regularly flown past Titan and the planet's other icy satellites. Like the Magellan

Venus probe, Cassini carries a powerful, cloud-penetrating radar. Cassini's radar observations of Titan have discovered several large seas and many lakes at its north pole. Titan is the only world in the Solar System other than Earth with standing bodies of liquid on its surface.

When Cassini flew past Saturn's sixth-largest moon, Enceladus, in 2005, it made another fascinating discovery. This bright white moon—one of the most reflective in the Solar System—was photographed with liquid water erupting in geysers from its south pole. As the liquid emerges into space, it freezes instantly, becoming a giant plume of ice crystals extending high above the moon's surface. Cassini scientists had discovered the source of Saturn's diffuse E Ring: it's continually being replenished by ice crystals from Enceladus. Because there is clearly a reservoir of liquid water under its surface, as with Jupiter's moon Europa, Enceladus was immediately considered a place potentially suitable for life.

In the spring 2007, Cassini was ordered to raise its orbit to follow a trajectory extending far above Saturn's poles. The result was one of the best planetary portraits ever taken. Seen from a position of about 700,000 miles above its north pole, the planet revealed the shady side of its complex ring system. More than enough sunlight filtered through those millions of icy, spinning fragments so that observers on Earth could see the rings in their full glory. On the opposite side of Saturn from the distant Sun, the shadow of the Solar System's second-largest planet fell like a black crescent on its immaculate rings.

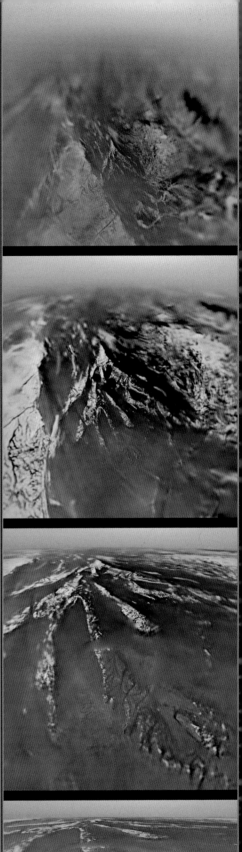
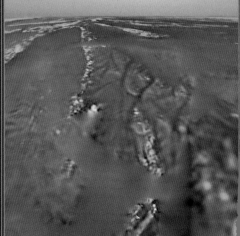

A spectacular view from an angle
high above Saturn's north pole.
We are looking at the unlit side
of the rings, but enough light
filters through them so that they
are clearly visible. Cassini, May 9,
2007.

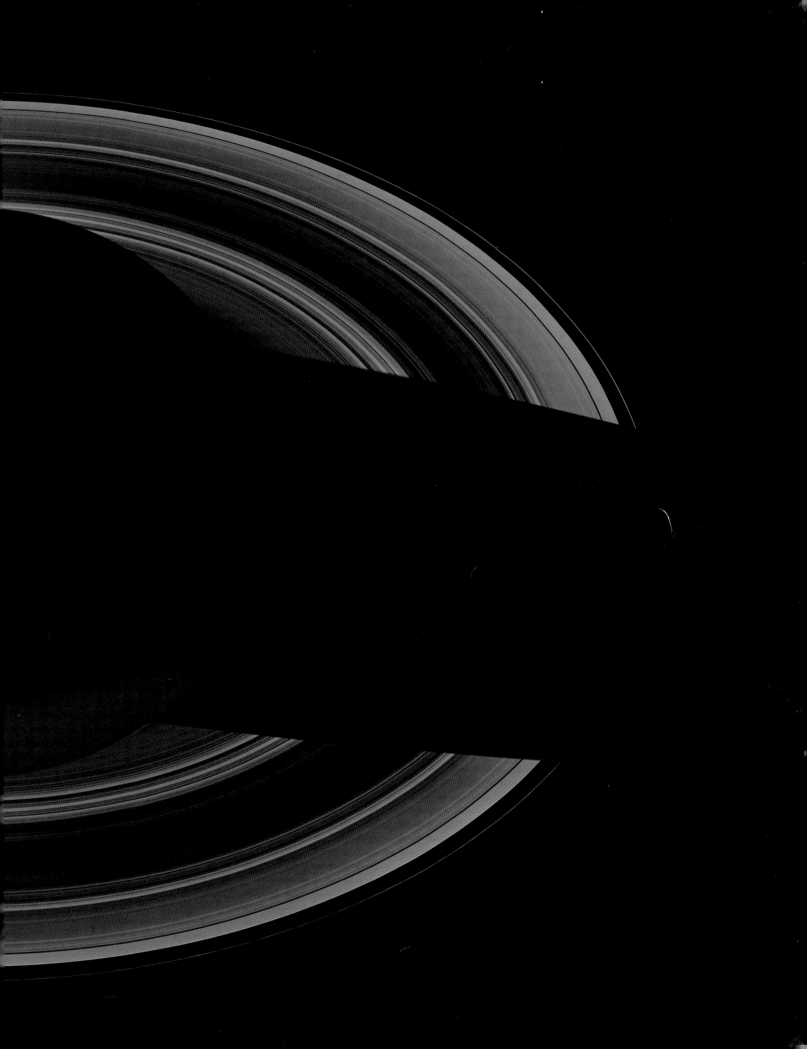

CHAPTER 10

URANUS

OPPOSITE **A polar view of immense, nearly featureless Uranus. A faint streak of pale clouds can be seen in the lower part of the planet, but that's all. The seventh planet from the Sun, Uranus has a circumference of 99,787 miles and completes an orbit around the Sun once every 84.3 years. Voyager 2, January 10, 1986.**

The third-largest planet and the third of the four gas giants, Uranus, is tipped on its side, with one pole pointing almost directly at the Sun and with its equator roughly aligned with the boundary between its day and its night hemispheres. This strangely off-kilter position, unique for a planet, is thought to be the result of a collision with another large body at an early stage of its development. Look for evidence of Uranus's idiosyncrasy, however, in the only available space probe pictures, and you will be disappointed. When Voyager 2 whipped past the planet on January 24, 1986, this sphere of hydrogen, helium, and methane was almost absolutely blank. Four times the diameter of the Earth and 20 times farther from the Sun, it was featureless to the point where the eye skated frictionlessly over its cool blue-green face (a color resulting from the small quantities of methane in its upper atmosphere, which absorb red light).

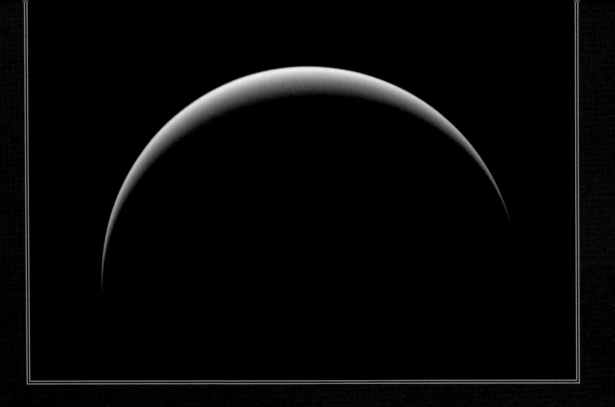

OPPOSITE **A south polar view of Uranus's moon Miranda. Miranda is the innermost and smallest of the five major Uranian satellites, just 300 miles in diameter. Multi-frame mosaic. Voyager 2, January 24, 1986.**

Although it has since been observed by the Hubble Space Telescope to have white clouds on occasion, in early 1986, Uranus had the quality of a purely abstract geometrical shape, as captured by Voyager 2. At that time, Uranus seemed to exist only to define its own form and to differentiate itself from the blackness in which it floated, and it didn't provide any more visual information than this, despite its size.

Like Venus, Uranus is frequently described as rotating in retrograde—meaning turning from east to west, backward compared to most of the Solar System's planets—but there is some dispute about which pole is the illuminated one, and which one is currently in darkness. (The two poles gradually switch their orientation every 42 years.) In any case, this debate shares some of the strangely slippery qualities of Uranus's visual featurelessness in 1986. Is there really any way to decide which is the north and which the south pole of a sideways planet that alternately points each pole at the

Sun? And how do you choose, without knowing which pole was "up," when the planet was knocked askance billions of years ago?

Because they have internal compositions and atmospheres somewhat different from their larger gas giant cousins Jupiter and Saturn, the two outermost planets—Uranus and Neptune—are sometimes put in a separate category by astronomers: they're called the "ice giants." Although, like its bigger relatives, Uranus is mostly made of hydrogen, it contains a much higher quantity of such elements as methane, water, and ammonia. These exist in the form of "ices." In the language of planetary science,

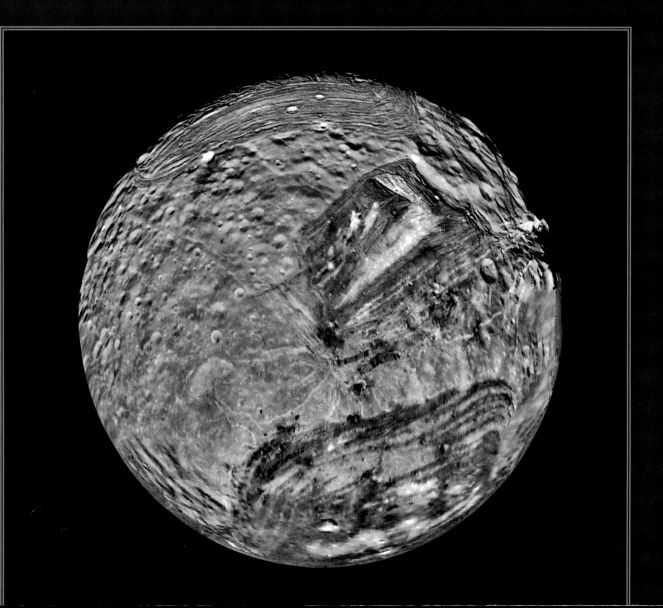

OPPOSITE This close view of Uranus's moon Miranda shows light and dark grooves with sharp boundaries. Voyager 2, January 24, 1986.

these ice forms don't necessarily mean something frozen but rather something that gradually transforms from being a gas at higher altitudes to something that sloshes around in liquid form when deeper inside the planet.

Uranus is very, very far away. At 1.78 billion miles from the Sun, it's far enough so that the signals of its flyby visitor Voyager 2 took two hours and 45 minutes to get to Earth—and that's at the speed of light. Not surprisingly, it's the first planet in this book that was unknown to the ancients. Although visible from Earth, it looks like a faint star, and is simply too slow-moving to be easily differentiated as a planet. The farther from the Sun a planet is, the slower it moves, and Uranus takes 84 Earth years to complete one orbit around the Sun (compare this to Mercury's 88 *days*). It was finally discovered by British astronomer William Herschel in 1781—though it had previously been noticed and catalogued by astronomers as a star.

Despite its record-breaking speed, Voyager 2, the only probe ever to visit Uranus, managed to get high-quality images of several of the planet's 21 moons. The most fascinating was Miranda—certainly one of the strangest moons beyond Jupiter. The smallest of Uranus's larger satellites and only one-sixth the size of the Earth's Moon, Miranda exhibits a bizarre terrain that includes faults and deep fracture lines. One theory holds that in the distant past Miranda was shattered into large fragments and then reassembled itself under the force of its own gravity. Like Jupiter and Neptune, Uranus also has a tenuous ring system—though no planet has rings to rival Saturn's.

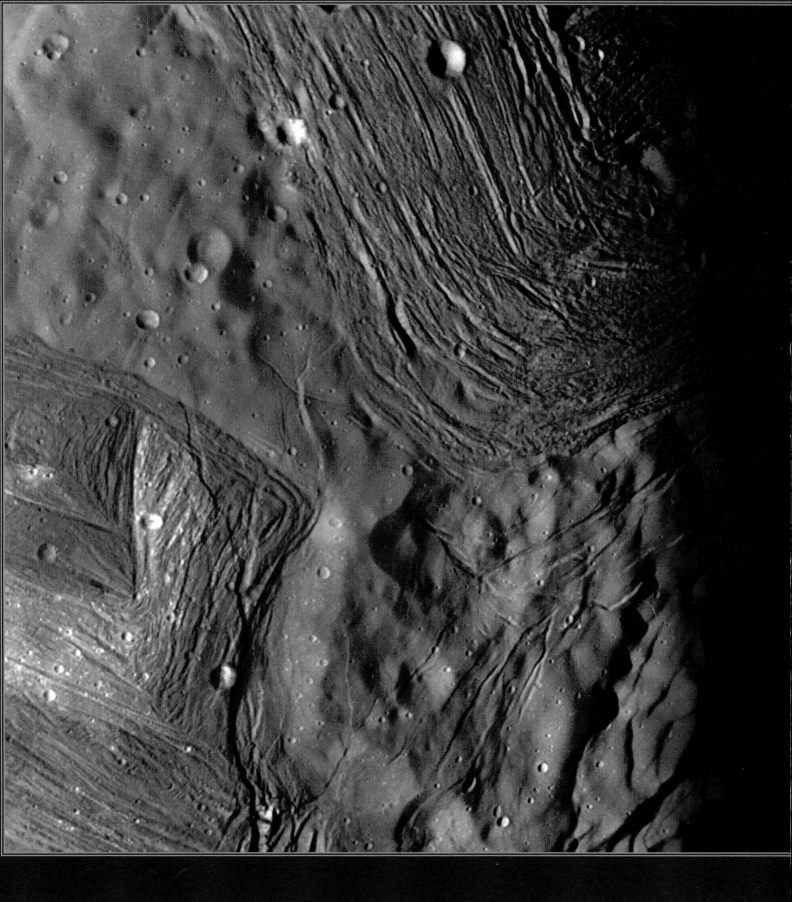

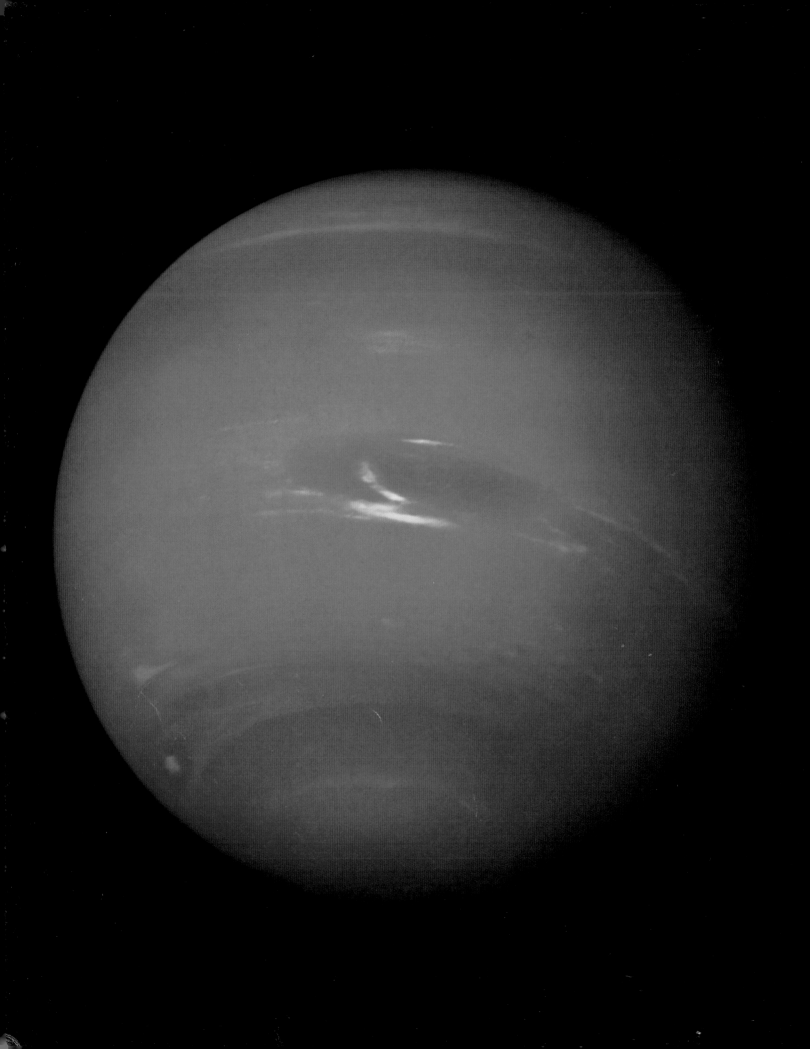

CHAPTER II

NEPTUNE

The submarine-blue planet Neptune, appropriately named after the Roman god of the sea, was the first planet found by mathematical predictions rather than by the telescope-assisted eye. Variations in Uranus's orbit led astronomers to believe that the gravity of an unknown eighth planet was tugging it. In September 1846, Neptune was found exactly at its predicted position.

Neptune is so far away that to it the Sun is only a very bright point of light in a sky swarming with other stars; so distant that by the time Voyager 2 arrived there in August 1989, its computers were 17 years old and most of its designers had retired; so removed that one might think it would be even more blank than Uranus, if only from the intense cold. The outermost planet, Neptune patrols the outskirts of the Solar System at an appropriately glacial pace, revolving around the Sun once every 165 years.

Instead of something as featureless as Uranus, however,

OPPOSITE **Neptune with its Great Dark Spot and its companion bright clouds. The eighth planet from the Sun, Neptune has a circumference of 96,683 miles and completes an orbit around the Sun once every 164.7 years. Voyager 2, August 19, 1989.**

OPPOSITE **In 1989, Neptune's southern hemisphere contained a disturbingly eyelike storm system, smaller than the dark spot. Voyager 2, August 23, 1989.**

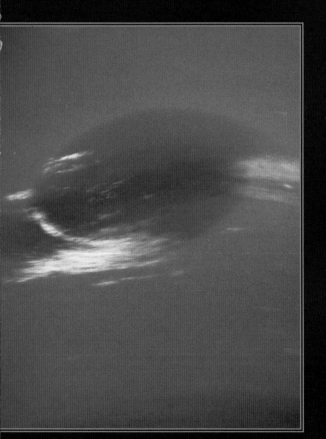

Voyager found one of the most intriguingly active of the giant outer planets. To begin with, from a distance Neptune looks eerily like the Earth—although, despite its name, its color isn't the result of water, but of the methane gas in its upper atmosphere. Like Jupiter and Saturn, but not Uranus, Neptune radiates more energy than it receives from the Sun, and therefore has some mysterious inner heat source. Viewed up close, it loses its Earthly appearance and starts to exhibit interesting features similar in some ways to those of the inner gas giants. Most notable, in 1989, was a vast bruise that was quickly called the Great Dark Spot, a swirling disturbance drifting in a position similar to that of Jupiter's Red Spot. Although its spiral shape and white clouds convinced scientists that it was a storm system, another theory holds that the Great Dark Spot is in fact an atmospheric depression—a hole in Neptune's methane clouds. Other intriguing features included a smaller dark spot with a disturbingly eyelike quality, and highly mobile white cirrus clouds, some of which were distended in vast streamers, casting shadows on lower parts of the atmosphere. Neptune's weather is easily as changeable as the Earth's, but on a far larger scale: the Great Dark Spot alone is about the size of Earth. And Neptune also appears to have the fastest winds in the Solar System, clocked by Voyager at an awesome 1,500 miles an hour (in contrast, the fastest winds on Earth are no more than 230 miles an hour).

Swift changes in Neptune's predominantly hydrogen atmosphere have persisted in the years since the Voyager

visible. It's possible that these rapid changes are driven by shifts in temperature; Neptune's powerful internal heat source may be creating updrafts that rise and mingle with frigid surface clouds that are as cold as –366° Fahrenheit. The various dark spots may also be the result of rising heat, which could be creating clear areas in the clouds; these in turn are thought to reveal lower, shaded cloud layers.

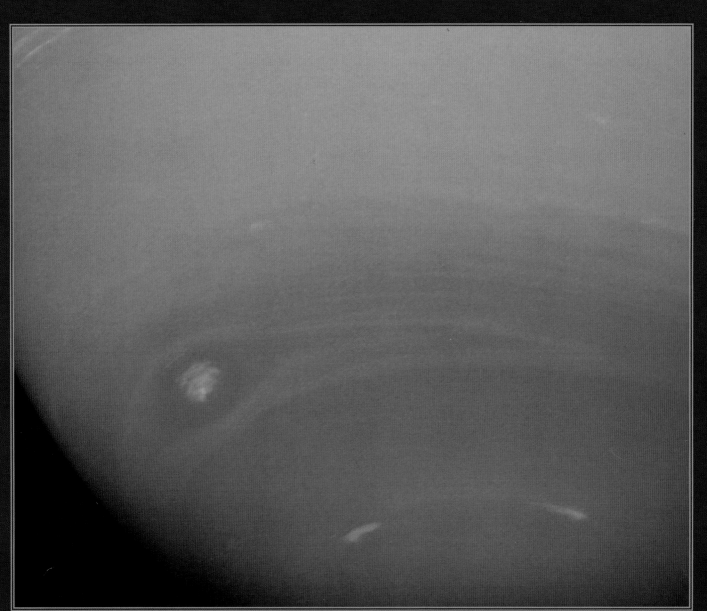

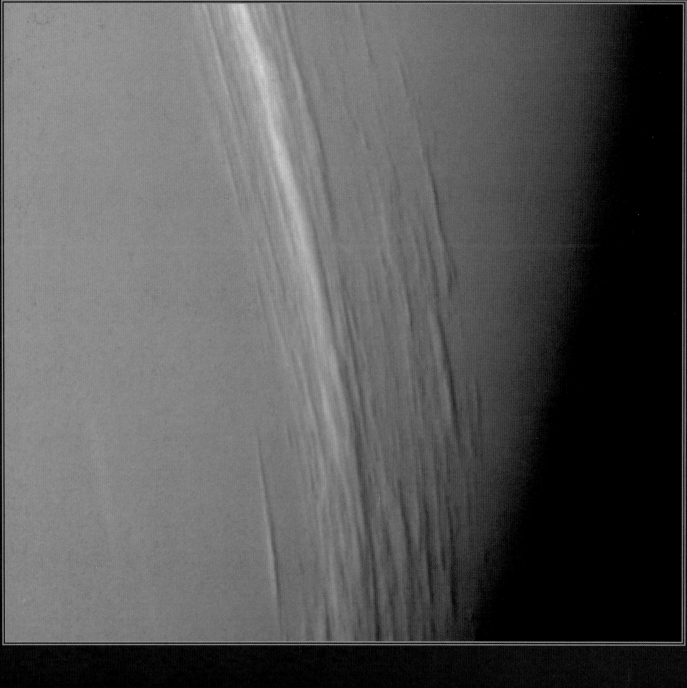

Just over five hours after Voyager buzzed by Neptune's
north pole at an altitude of 3,000 miles—the closest of
its four planetary approaches—it swung past Triton, the
largest of Neptune's moons and the seventh largest in the
Solar System. Triton proved to be one of the most startling
objects in the sky. At –391° Fahrenheit, this moon is the
coldest place ever directly observed in nature, so you might

expect it to be little more than a cratered lump of icy rock. Instead, it's comparable to Jupiter's moon Io in many ways, with a young surface almost completely unmarked by craters and an extremely thin atmosphere that even supports faint polar clouds. Its atmosphere appeared to be partially maintained by icy plumes of what seemed to be black nitrogen gas. Voyager revealed Triton to be one of only five Solar System objects known to support active volcanism, with the others being Earth, Venus, Jupiter's moon Io, and Saturn's moon Enceladus. (In the case of Triton and Enceladus, however, these are cold eruptions due to *cryovolcanism*, or ice volcanoes.) Voyager photographs revealed several of them visibly spewing material about five miles above the surface. This was an entirely unexpected vision, though it fit well with the long list of other surprises that the two Voyagers had provided about the four giant outer planets and their diverse moons.

Voyager 2's flyby of Neptune and Triton concluded with a series of pictures in which the moon could be seen orbiting beside the planet's deep blue crescent as the pair rapidly receded behind the speeding spacecraft. Then this intricate machine, which had traveled 4.5 billion miles in the 12 years since its launch, shot into the inky nothingness at the edge of the Solar System. Its tour of the outer planets concluded, it was soon ordered to turn its camera systems off forever. Although several of its instruments remain switched on and the probe continues to send data to Earth, Voyager's astonishing flood of interplanetary visions had finally ceased.

OPPOSITE **A vertical relief in Neptune's bright cloud streaks. Voyager 2, August 24, 1989.**

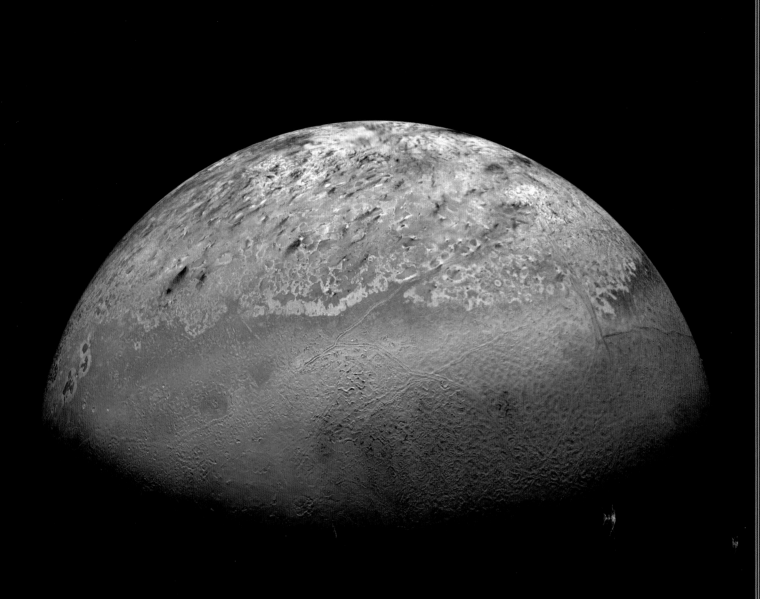

Neptune's icy moon Triton has the
coldest surface known anywhere
in the Solar System, about −391°
Fahrenheit. Dark streaks are
believed to have been deposited
from huge geyserlike plumes, some
of which were active when Voyager
flew by. Multi-frame mosaic.
Voyager 2, August 25, 1989.

A dual crescent view of Neptune and its moon Triton (at bottom). Voyager 2, August 31, 1989.

he last 50 years have seen an unprecedented explosion of information about our Solar System, the Milky Way, and the galaxies beyond. For the first time in human history, other worlds have truly become *real* to us: places with mountains, deserts, volcanoes, oceans, seas, clouds, and rain. And this knowledge can only help us understand our own world and our place in the greater frame of the cosmos. We are also discovering more and more planets around other stars—though we don't yet know much about them.

The question is, what will we do with our increasing body of knowledge? How will it help us to better grapple with our problems here on Earth? If we fail to act, will our blue-white home world continue heating up and possibly start to slowly resemble super-hot Venus, a broiling planet with a thick, stifling atmosphere? Or might it eventually go the opposite way and end up similar to Mars—a frozen

OPPOSITE Sea life may well exist under the frozen, fissured surface of Jupiter's moon Europa—we won't know until we land there to see. This mosaic covers a large part of the northern hemisphere and includes the north pole at the top of the image. Galileo, June 27, 1996.

desert world that's lost most of its atmosphere? Either fate might seem unlikely—and yet both of these planets are thought to once have had oceans and maybe even life. Sound familiar?

Of course, if there is a single, very big question behind all of the space missions thus far, it is: Are we alone in the Universe? Or does life exist elsewhere? We simply don't know yet—but we may be getting closer to an answer. And as someone once commented: either way, the answer would be equally astonishing.

The good news is that we've become better and better at using the limited amount of money that is being spent on space exploration. As a result, for little more than the budget of a major Hollywood movie each—about $400 million—two robot landscape photographers, also known as rovers, are still crawling across the rusty deserts of Mars, more than four years after their arrival. Low-budget probes are also currently on their way to visit Mercury and Pluto, and smaller objects such as asteroids and comets will also be visited in the next 10 years. About 20 space probes are currently active, with more on the way. The school bus–size Cassini Orbiter continues to wheel among the moons and rings of Saturn, and it should continue doing so for at least another two years and perhaps many more. NASA is also planning a large-scale mission to study Jupiter's moon Europa, which almost certainly contains a vast liquid water ocean under its ice.

Twenty missions sounds like a lot—and yet we could be doing more. There has never been a better time to become

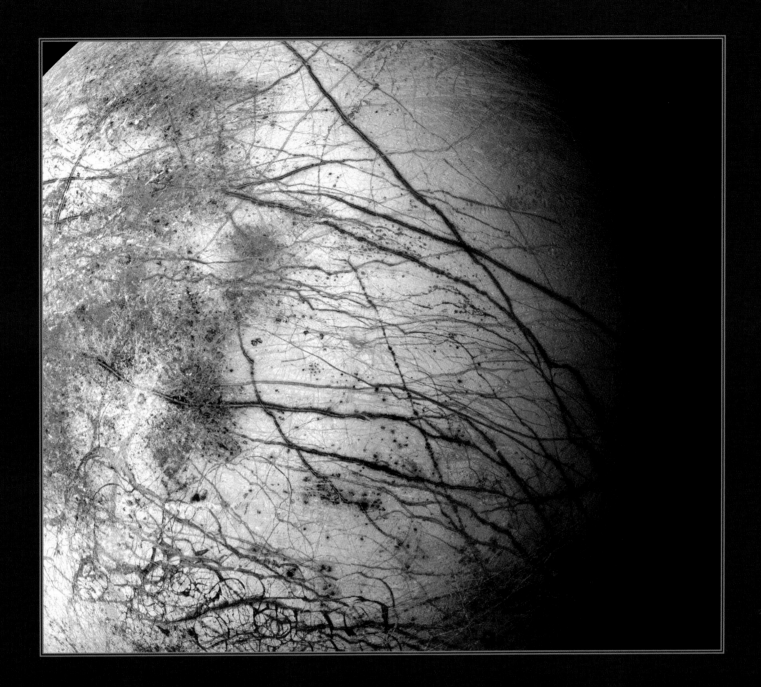

an astronomer or planetary scientist, and it has never been more urgent that we have good ones. If this book serves to interest some of its readers in the astonishing process of discovery that has led us to our current understanding of our Solar System and the greater Galaxy and Universe, I'll be well satisfied. And if some eventually choose to pursue careers as astronomers or planetary scientists, I'll be happier still.

GLOSSARY

ASTEROID Also sometimes called a minor planet or even a "planetoid," an asteroid is a body in the Solar System that is smaller than a planet or a dwarf planet but larger than a meteoroid. (Meteoroids are sometimes defined as being 10 meters across or less.)

ASTRONOMY The study of celestial objects (such as planets, moons, asteroids, comets, stars, and galaxies) and phenomena outside the Earth's atmosphere. Astronomy is concerned with the formation and development of the Universe and the physics, chemistry, meteorology, evolution, and motion of celestial objects.

ATMOSPHERE A layer of gases that surrounds a celestial body such as a planet or moon.

CELESTIAL Something of or related to the sky.

CENTRIFUGAL FORCE A force that pulls a rotating, or spinning, object away from the center of its spin. Artificial gravity can be produced using centrifugal force. A good example of centrifugal force is when water stays at the bottom of a bucket if it is spun in a circle fast enough.

COMET A comet is a small, icy Solar System body that orbits the Sun and exhibits a visible tail, or atmosphere, when it nears the Sun. The tail, which extends out from a comet in a direction opposite the Sun, comes from the effects of solar radiation upon the comet's nucleus, which is usually made of ice, dust, and rocks and measures a few miles to tens of miles across.

COSMOS Although in its most general definition a cosmos is any orderly system, in fact the word is generally used as a synonym of the word *universe*.

CRYOVOLCANO A cryovolcano is an icy volcano. Cryovolcanoes form on icy moons such as Saturn's moon Enceladus and Neptune's moon Triton, and possibly on other low-temperature astronomical objects. Rather than molten rock, these volcanoes erupt icy volatiles such as ammonia, methane, or water. Referred to as cryomagma, or ice-volcanic melt, these substances are usually liquids and form plumes, but they can also be in the form of vapors.

DWARF PLANET A dwarf planet is a celestial body orbiting the Sun that is massive enough to be rounded by its own gravity but which has not pushed away its neighboring smaller Solar System bodies (such as asteroids) and is not a natural satellite. A dwarf planet has to have enough mass for its own gravity to force it into a spherical or near-spherical shape. "Dwarf planet" was only approved as a category by the International Astronomical Union in 2006, and was applied to Pluto, previously considered a planet.

GALAXY A galaxy is a massive system that is bound together by its own gravity and that consists of stars, interstellar gas and dust, and a substance called dark matter that is not yet well understood. Galaxies come in many different forms, including spiral and elliptical. The Earth and its Solar System are within the Milky Way Galaxy, which we know to be spiral shaped.

GAS A state of matter consisting of a collection of elementary particles such as molecules, atoms, ions, and electrons that is without a fixed volume or shape and is in more or less random motion. The Earth's atmosphere is made up of a gas that consists of mostly nitrogen and oxygen.

GAS GIANT A large planet that is not primarily composed of solid matter such as rock or ice but which rather is largely composed of gases. The Solar System has four gas giants: Jupiter, Saturn, Uranus, and Neptune. In recent years many other gas giants have been discovered around other stars in the Milky Way.

GRAVITY One of the fundamental forces of physics, gravity is a natural phenomenon by which all objects with mass attract each other. It is also known as gravitation. In everyday life, gravitation is most commonly thought of as the force that gives objects weight: it is because of gravity that if you drop something, it falls to the ground. But gravity is also responsible for keeping the Earth and the other planets in orbit around the Sun, and for keeping the Moon in orbit around the Earth. The gravity of the Moon and the Sun produces tides, and gravity can also heat the interiors of stars and planets to very high temperatures as they form. The gravitational interactions of Jupiter and its large moons are thought to be one reason why Jupiter's moon Europa probably has a large ocean of liquid water under its ice.

MASS In physics the mass of an object is one measure by which the amount of matter in that object is gauged. In everyday usage, mass is more commonly referred to as weight. In physics and engineering, however, weight means the strength of the gravitational pull on an object, or how heavy it is as measured in various units of force. But mass is actually an inertial property, meaning it is independent of gravity or other forces. Weight is the force created when a mass is acted upon by a gravitational field. In everyday situations, the weight of an object is proportional to its mass, which usually makes it unproblematic to use the same word for both concepts.

MESOPOTAMIA From the Ancient Greek meaning "the land between the two rivers," Mesopotamia is an area between the Tigris and Euphrates Rivers, located geographically in what now largely corresponds to modern Iraq, southeastern Turkey, northeastern Syria, and southwestern Iran. Mesopotamia is where the first settled human communities are known to have formed, and where the first writing developed.

METEOROID Known as a meteor when it enters the Earth's atmosphere, a meteoroid is a particle of debris in the Solar System that can range in size from a boulder to a piece of sand. The definition of a meteoroid from the International Astronomical Union is "a solid object moving in interplanetary space, of a size considerably smaller than an asteroid and considerably larger than an atom." Meteoroids are sometimes defined as being 10 meters across or less. The visible path of a meteoroid that enters the atmosphere of the Earth or another planet is commonly called a "shooting star" or a "falling star." Meteoroids are regularly found on Earth, and have also been spotted on the surface of Mars by NASA rovers.

MOON While we call our natural satellite *the* Moon, in fact a moon is any natural satellite of a planet or smaller body.

ORBIT In physics, an orbit is the path an object takes around a point or another body. All of the Solar System's planets orbit the Sun.

PLANET A celestial body that has cleared its neighboring region of the smaller objects, known as planetesimals, is in orbit around a star or a stellar remnant, and is massive enough that its shape is rounded by its own gravity, but is not massive enough to cause thermonuclear fusion. A planet can clear its orbit of planetesimals either by absorbing them or by forcing them into other orbits.

PLANETARY SCIENCE Also known as planetology and closely related to planetary astronomy, it is the science of planets and planetary systems, and the Solar System. A team of planetary scientists is usually attached to every mission by a space probe.

PLANETESIMAL A small solid object thought to have orbited the Sun during the formation of the planets 4.5 billion years ago. Planetesimals are thought to have come together to form the planets and moons or to have evolved into such objects as asteroids, comets, and meteoroids.

POLE A pole is either end of a planet, moon, or Sun at the axis of rotation.

ROBOT A robot is a mechanical or a virtual device. It is usually a mechanical system that, by its visual appearance or movements, conveys a sense that it has an intent of its own. The word "robot" can refer to both physical robots and to virtual software agents. The latter are usually referred to as "bots" to differentiate between the two.

ROCKET A rocket or rocket vehicle is a missile or other vehicle that obtains thrust by the ejection of a fast-moving gas or fluid from its engine. All space probes have been launched into space by rockets.

SATELLITE A satellite is either an object that has been placed into orbit by human beings or a natural object, such as a moon, orbiting a planet. Mechanical satellites are sometimes called artificial satellites to distinguish them from natural ones.

SCIENCE The effort to understand how the physical world works, with observable physical evidence used as the basis of that understanding. The scientific method relies on the observation of phenomena and/or experimentation that simulates phenomena under controlled conditions.

SCIENTIST Any person engaged in systematic scientific research to acquire knowledge about the physical world.

SEASON One of a planet's different periodic meteorological times of year. Seasons are determined by a planet's position relative to the Sun and can vary between planetary hemispheres. Some planetary seasons are a result of the tilt in a planet's axis, which results in differing durations of exposure of that planet's hemispheres to the Sun, and some are a result of a planet's changing distance from the Sun during its orbit.

SOLAR SYSTEM Our Solar System consists of the Sun and all the celestial objects that are bound to it by gravity. These objects include the eight planets and their 166 known moons; five dwarf planets and their six known moons; and billions of small bodies, including asteroids, comets, and meteors.

SPACE A boundless three-dimensional extent or expanse in which all matter exists and all objects and events occur and have a position and direction relative to each other. The Solar System, the Milky Way Galaxy, and all other known galaxies exist in space. Space is sometimes defined as the entire region beyond the Earth's atmosphere and all

it contains, but in fact the Earth is also a part of space.

SPACE PROBE A robotic vehicle used in space exploration missions, usually for scientific purposes. Space probes leave the gravity of Earth and approach the Moon or enter interplanetary or even interstellar space.

STAR A star is a massive, luminous ball of energy. The nearest star to Earth is our Sun, which is the source of most of the energy on Earth. There are billions of stars in the Milky Way Galaxy. Most are between 1 billion and 10 billion years old, but some are thought to be close to 13.7 billion years old, which is the observable age of the Universe. Our Sun is 4.57 billion years old.

TERRESTRIAL PLANET A planet that is primarily composed of rocks, as opposed to the gas giant planets, which are primarily made of gas. The terrestrial planets in our Solar System are also the closest planets to the Sun: Mercury, Venus, Earth, and Mars.

TRAJECTORY The path an object follows as it moves through space. Such an object might be a rocket or a space probe, for example.

UNIVERSE The Universe is commonly defined as everything that exists: the entirety of space and time; all types of matter, energy, and momentum; and the physical laws and constants that govern them. Observations by astronomers indicate that the Universe is about 13.7 billion years old and at least 93 billion light-years across.

VOLCANO A volcano is an opening in a planet's surface crust, which allows molten rock and hot ash and gases to escape from below the surface. Over time, volcanic activity involving the extrusion, or pushing out, of molten rock tends to form mountains or features like mountains. The highest mountain in the Solar System, Olympus Mons, is a dormant volcano on Mars. It is almost 17 miles high. Many active volcanoes exist on Jupiter's moon Io.

A Note on the Pictures

My intention with this book was to present a selection from the most compelling photographs taken during 50 years of robotic spaceflight. My choices were always in response to the visual qualities of an image—to find the most evocative, compelling pictures and present them as photographs first. I also wanted to give the reader a sense of what it might like to actually *be there*. I strongly believe the remarkable photographic legacy of these space missions constitutes a valuable chapter in the history of photography as much as it belongs to astronomy or the planetary sciences. Each of the spacecraft is credited at the end of the caption accompanying its picture, along with the date on which it took that picture.

Some of these pictures came directly from such NASA Web sites as Planetary Photojournal and were simply cleaned up digitally to better prepare them for high-quality printing. Others were the result of patient searches through the many tens of thousands of raw frames archived at such comprehensive Web sites as the PDS Imaging Node, a site in which the complete visual record of NASA's missions is presented. (See Web site addresses in the Select Bibliography section.) Quite a few of the pictures in the book are mosaics of many individual frames, which I assembled from such raw images and then further processed. Such composite images are clearly identified in the captions. Of these, the color data in the color mosaics was prepared with the invaluable help of Dr. Paul Geissler of the U.S. Geological Survey. A number of these images used unorthodox wavelengths of light, or even invisible electromagnetic pulses of radar, in order to be produced. For example, some images record the Sun's X-rays, rather than its visible light, and one picture of Venus used ultraviolet light to produce a better view of that planet's clouds than would be possible with regular visible light. All such images are labeled. And a few of these shots came from such brilliant individual image processors as Calvin J. Hamilton and Gordan Ugarkovic, whose cooperation and contribution is much appreciated. Finally, all of these images ultimately came about as a result of decades of patient, creative work by many thousands of planetary scientists and engineers both inside and outside of NASA, ESA (the European Space Agency), and JAXA (the Japanese Aerospace Exploration Agency). Their pathbreaking work is humbly acknowledged here.

One final note on the selection of pictures in this book. Astute readers will notice two categories of Solar System objects not represented here: comets and dwarf planets. Dwarf planets, which now include Pluto, reflect a new category of Solar System objects, which was agreed to by the International Astronomical Union in 2006.

The reason for the exclusion of comet and dwarf planet images was a lack of truly good photographs of these objects. While many pictures of comets do exist, few were taken by robotic spacecraft, and of these, none quite meet the standards of this book. (Most of the pictures printed here were taken by space probes.)

Happily, this problem should be corrected within a few years. In 2014, the European Space Agency's Rosetta space probe, which carries a superb camera system, should encounter comet 67P/Churyumov-Gerasimenko. Rosetta will even drop a lander on the comet. The following year, the NASA spacecraft New Horizons will fly past the dwarf planet Pluto and its large moon Charon. The NASA craft carries an excellent camera system, too. After Pluto, New Horizons will proceed much farther into space, with the mission of taking photographs of one or more of the mysterious (and very distant) Kuiper Belt Objects, or KBOs. These small icy bodies, thought to be made of frozen methane, ammonia, and water, represent another class of Solar System objects that we currently have very little knowledge about and no good photographs of—yet.

—M.B.

Select Bibliography

Books

Coming of Age in the Milky Way. Timothy Ferris. William Morrow, 1988.

Cosmos. Carl Sagan. Random House, 1980.

Greetings, Carbon-Based Bipeds! Arthur C. Clarke. St Martin's Press, 1999.

Mapping Mars: Science, Imagination, and the Birth of a World. Oliver Morton. Picador, 2002.

Pale Blue Dot: A Vision of the Human Future in Space. Carl Sagan. Random House, 1994.

The Planets. Dava Sobel. Viking, 2005.

Satellites of the Outer Planets: Worlds in Their Own Right. David A. Rothery. Oxford University Press, 1999.

The Whole Shebang: A State-of-the-Universe(s) Report. Timothy Ferris. Simon & Schuster, 1997.

Web Sites

Planetary Photojournal **photojournal.jpl.nasa.gov/index.html**

Views of the Solar System **www.solarviews.com/eng/homepage.htm**

Unmanned Spaceflight **www.unmannedspaceflight.com/**

The Nine Planets Solar System Tour **www.nineplanets.org/**

PDS Imaging Node **pds-imaging.jpl.nasa.gov**

Visible Earth **visibleearth.nasa.gov/**

NASA Images **www.nasaimages.org**

PICTURE CREDITS

Note: In these credits, "MB, KP" stands for "Michael Benson, Kinetikon Pictures," and "PG" stands for "Dr. Paul Geissler."

Jacket front cover: NASA/JPL Space Science Institute/MB, KP. Jacket spine: NASA/Johns Hopkins University Applied Physics Laboratory/Carnegie Institution of Washington/MB, KP. Jacket back cover: NASA/JPL/MB, KP. Jacket back flap: NASA/JPL/MB, KP. Book case front cover: ESA/DLR/FU Berlin (G. Neukum)/MB, KP. Book case spine: NASA/JPL/Cassini Imaging Team/MB, KP. Book case back cover: NASA/JPL/MB, KP. Page vi: Carnegie Science Center, Pittsburgh. Page 2: Wikimedia Commons. Page 3: NASA/MB, KP. Page 4: Miha Tursic. Page 5: Miha Tursic. Page 7: Kuyunjik Collection, British Museum, London. Page 9: Harmonia Macrocosmica by Andreas Cellarius. Page 11: Harmonia Macrocosmica by Andreas Cellarius. Page 13, above: Collection of the author. Page 13, below: Courtesy of Adler Planetarium and Astronomy Museum, Chicago, Illinois. Page 14: Portrait of Galileo Galilei by Justus Sustermans (1597–1681), Wikimedia Commons. Page 15: Collection of the author. Page 18: United States Naval Observatory Library. Page 19: NASA. Page 20: NASA. Page 21: Miha Tursic. Page 22: NASA/Johns Hopkins University Applied Physics Laboratory/Carnegie Institution of Washington/MB, KP. Pages 24–25: The SeaWiFS project, NASA/Goddard, and Orbimage. Page 27: NASA/JPL/MB, KP. Page 28: NASA RPIF/PG/MB, KP. Page 29: NASA RPIF/PG/MB, KP. Page 30: Jeff Schmaltz; MODIS/NASA/GSFC/MB, KP. Page 31: The SeaWiFS project, NASA/Goddard, and Orbimage. Pages 32–33, above series: MB, KP. Pages 32–33, below: NASA/JPL/MB, KP. Page 35: NASA/Calvin J. Hamilton. Page 36: NASA/JPL/USGS/MB, KP. Page 38: Courtesy of Donald P. Mitchell and the Russian Space Program. Page 39: NASA/JPL/USGS/MB. Page 40: ESA/NASA/MB, KP. Page 42: ESA/NASA/MB, KP. Page 43: NASA/Stanford-Lockheed Institute/MB, KP. Page 44: NASA/Stanford-Lockheed Institute/MB, KP. Page 45: SOHO (ESA and NASA)/MB, KP. Page 47: ISASS Japan/JAXA Japanese space agency/Lockheed Martin Palo Alto Research Center. Page 49: TRACE, Stanford-Lockheed Institute/NASA/MB, KP. Page 51: NASA/Mark S. Robinson; Mercury 1. Pages 52–53: NASA/Calvin Hamilton/MB, KP. Page 54: MPS for OSIRIS Team MPS/UPD/LAM/IAA/RSSD/INTA/UPM/DASP/IDA/MB, KP. Page 57: NASA/JPL/MB, KP. Page 58: NASA/JPL/PG/MB, KP. Page 59: ESA/DLR/FU Berlin (G. Neukum). Pages 60–61: NASA/JPL/MB, KP. Pages 62–63: NASA/JPL/PG/MB, KP. Pages 64–65: NASA/JPL/MB, KP. Page 66, above: NASA/JPL/MB, KP. Pages 66–67, below: NASA/JPL/MB, KP. Page 68: NASA/Mark S. Robinson, Northwestern University/MB, KP. Page 71: NASA/JPL/MB, KP. Page 72, above: NASA/Johns Hopkins University/MB, KP. Page 72, below: NASA/Mark S. Robinson/MB, KP. Page 74: NASA/Johns Hopkins University/MB, KP. Page 75: NASA/Mark S. Robinson, Northwestern University/MB, KP. Page 77: NASA/JPL/Cassini Imaging Team/MB, KP. Page 79: NASA/JPL/MB, KP. Pages 80–81: NASA/JPL/MB, KP. Page 82: NASA/JPL/MB, KP. Page 83: NASA/JPL/MB, KP. Pages 84–85: NASA/JPL/MB, KP. Page 86: NASA/JPL/PIRL/University of Arizona/MB, KP. Page 87: NASA/JPL/Ciclops/University of Arizona/MB, KP. Page 88: NASA/JPL/Gordon Ugarkovic. Page 90: NASA/JPL/Gordan Ugarkovic. Page 91: NASA/JPL/Space Science Institute/MB, KP. Page 92: NASA/JPL/MB, KP. Page 93: NASA/JPL/Gordon Ugarkovic. Page 94: NASA/JPL/Space Science Institute/MB, KP. Page 95: ESA/NASA/JPL/University or Arizona/MB, KP. Pages 96–97: NASA/JPL/Space Science Institute/MB, KP. Page 99: NASA/JPL/Calvin J. Hamilton. Page 100: NASA/JPL. Page 101: NASA/JPL/USGS/MB, KP. Page 103: NASA/JPL/Calvin J. Hamilton. Page 104: NASA/JPL/MB, KP. Page 106: NASA/JPL/MB, KP. Page 107: NASA/JPL/MB, KP. Page 108: NASA/JPL/MB, KP. Page 110: NASA/JPL/MB, KP. Page 111: NASA/JPL/MB, KP/Acknowledgement: Calvin Hamilton. Page 113: MPS for OSIRIS Team MPS/UPD/LAM/MB, KP. Page 115: NASA/JPL/USGS/MB, KP.

INDEX

BOOK CASE FRONT COVER A view of the complex caldera at the summit of Olympus Mons on Mars, the highest volcano in the Solar System. Olympus Mons has an elevation of almost 15 miles relative to the surrounding surface, and the caldera has a depth of almost 2 miles. Mars Express, January 21, 2004.

BOOK CASE BACK COVER Martian clouds and atmosphere. Viking Orbiter 1, January 15, 1978.

Library of Congress Cataloging-in-Publication Data

Benson, Michael.
Beyond : a solar system voyage / By Michael Benson.
p. cm.
ISBN 978-0-8109-8322-9
1. Solar system. 2. Solar system—Pictorial works. 3. Astronomy—Pictorial works.
I. Title.
QB501.B46 2009
523.2—dc22
2008022297

Text copyright © 2009 Michael Benson
Book design by Maria T. Middleton
Space probe icons by Miha Tursic
For picture credits, see page 119.

Printed and bound in China
10 9 8 7 6 5 4 3 2 1

Abrams Books for Young Readers are available at special discounts when purchased in quantity for premiums and promotions as well as fundraising or educational use. Special editions can also be created to specification. For details, contact specialmarkets@hnabooks.com or the address below.

HNA
harry n. abrams, inc.
a subsidiary of La Martinière Groupe
115 West 18th Street
New York, NY 10011
www.hnabooks.com